THE BEST OF

COUNTRY

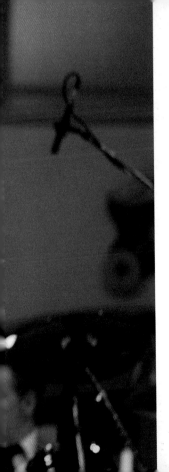

THE BEST OF

COUNTRY

The Essential CD Guide

Stacy Harris

CollinsPublishersSanFrancisco

A Division of HarperCollins*Publishers*

This book is dedicated to Lloyd, Francine, Sue, Mike, Michael, Blake, Ross and Whitney.

First published in the United States in 1993 by Collins Publishers San Francisco,
1160 Battery Street, San Francisco, California 94111

Text and Design copyright © 1993 by Carlton Books Limited, London
CD Guide format copyright © 1993 Carlton Books Limited
The Essential CD Guides is a registered trademark

Library of Congress Cataloging-in-Publication Data

Harris, Stacy.
  The best of country : the essential CD guide / Stacy Harris.
        p.   cm. — (The Essential CD guides)
  Discography: p.
  Includes bibliographical references and index.
  ISBN 0-00-255335-X
  1. Country musicians—United States—Biography—Dictionaries.
  2. Compact discs—Reviews.   I. Title.   II. Series.
  ML 102.C7H38   1993
  781.642—dc20   93-11542
                                                              CIP
                                                              MN
Printed in Great Britain

THE AUTHOR

Stacy Harris is an internationally known columnist, broadcast journalist,
feature writer, lecturer and arts critic who covers the Nashville entertainment
scene for the ABC radio network's 2,000 affiliated stations. An editor for
Country Song Roundup, *Country Spirit* and *Spotlight on Country* magazines, Stacy
Harris's writing has also appeared in *Billboard*, *US*, *Entertainment Weekly*,
Goldmine, *Country Music People* and *Country Music*. She is the author of *Comedians
of Country Music* and *The Carter Family* (both published by Lerner).

Contents

INTRODUCTION

White Man's Blues

✪ ✪ ✪

"**I**F IT SOUNDS COUNTRY, THAT'S WHAT IT IS." THAT'S HOW KRIS KRISTOFFERSON ANSWERS THE AGE-OLD QUESTION "WHAT IS COUNTRY MUSIC?" HISTORICAL SUMMARIES ARE, BY VIRTUE OF SPACE LIMITATIONS, INCOMPLETE. SIMILARLY, EVEN INFORMED OPINION IS PURELY SUBJECTIVE. WITH THOSE DISCLAIMERS, LET'S FORGE AHEAD.

Musicologists define country music as a genre rooted in the folk music of England, Ireland and Scotland. America's first settlers brought their ballads, fiddle tunes, jigs and reels—folk songs and dance music passed on from generation to generation—with them. Religious music, typified by hymns and other sacred songs, was also a part of their heritage. (This tradition continues through the popularity of gospel-flavored country songs.) As times changed, so did the music, reflecting the experiences of a working-class, often rural population, and also the "white man's blues" of an upwardly-mobile nation of immigrants.

During the late 1800s, stringed instruments were introduced to what was then called folk music. One of the most popular was the banjo, an instrument of African origin, brought to the New World by slaves and played nearly exclusively by blacks until around 1850. The guitar, an import from London drawing rooms, is older than the banjo but gained acceptance only after the banjo was established. Later the mandolin and steel guitar would become as closely identified with the sound of country as these two "pioneers."

As traveling minstrel and medicine shows were joined by vaudeville, the popularity and growth of what would become known as country music became apparent. In 1871, Kentucky songwriter Will Hays wrote a song called 'The Little Old Log Cabin In The Lane'. It would be one of earliest songs ever recorded, some 53 years later, when Fiddlin' John Carson, a 55-year-old Georgia radio performer, recorded it. (Another fiddler, Eck Robertson, recorded 'Sallie Gooden' on July 1, 1922 while Robertson and Henry Gilliland recorded the first discs ever made by Southern country musicians a day earlier.)

In 1924 Vernon Dalhart recorded 'The Prisoner's Song,' the best-selling, pre-electric recording. By 1925, the art form now known as country music was generally being referred to as hillbilly. On November 25 of that same year, the *Grand Ole Opry* began its run on WSM Radio as the longest continuously-running radio stage show in history. Uncle Jimmy Thompson, an 85-year-old fiddler, was the first to perform on the Opry stage.

In 1927, the (original) Carter Family signed a 5-year recording contract. Their impact was such that the so-called "Golden Age of Country Music" was said to have ended when they retired in 1943. The man who discovered the trio, talent scout Ralph Peer, also signed Jimmie Rodgers, who sold more than 20 million records during his brief career.

All told, more than 50,000 country songs were released prior to the Second World War, due in part to the popularity of radio barn dances. The most famous of these were WLS's *National Barn Dance*, Louisville's *Renfro Valley Barn Dance*, Richmond, Virginia's *Old Dominion Barn Dance* and Shreveport's *Louisiana Hayride*. Today, only West Virginia's *Wheeling Jamboree* endures.

Those who enjoyed barn dances, south-eastern folk music and western cowboy music were, by the Forties, dropping coins in juke-boxes to hear western swing and, later, honky-tonk music as well.

Bob Wills, Al Dexter and Spade Cooley led the list of Forties western swing greats, while honky-tonk heroes of that decade included Ted Daffan, Floyd Tillman and Moon Mullican, "the King of the Hillbilly Piano-Players." The Second World War prompted Elton Britt to record 'There's A Star Spangled Banner Waving Somewhere' in 1942. This number became country music's first gold record.

Lefty Frizzell, Hank Williams and Johnny Horton continued the honky-tonk tradition in the Fifties when the emergence of rock 'n' roll seemed to sound the death knell for country music.

Nashville was on its way to becoming "Music City USA" and the home of the Nashville sound. Roy Acuff and Fred Rose had established Nashville's first music publishing company, Acuff-Rose, in 1943 and

Sheb Wooley recorded in a makeshift recording studio set up in a small, WSM radio studio 2 years later. Owen Bradley's famed Quonset Hut was set up in 1955, and by 1960 Bradley and Chet Atkins were beginning to produce a succession of hit country records. Some of these "crossed over" and were played on rock 'n' roll radio stations, continuing a pattern established years earlier by Eddy Arnold and others, whose country records were played on the popular music stations of the day.

The trend continued, albeit sporadically, through the Sixties and Seventies. In 1980, the movie *Urban Cowboy* heightened interest in country music, bringing its artists larger record sales and greater media recognition—but some of the Eighties gains proved to have all of the staying power of a fad. Not so in the Nineties where, thanks to George Strait, Randy Travis and Clint Black before him, "the Garth Brooks phenomenon" has made country one of America's most popular music formats.

COWBOY SONGS

Musical Preservation of the Cowboy Legacy

CATEGORIZING THE SOUNDS OF COUNTRY IS A MONUMENTAL TASK. ARE SOME CATEGORIES REDUNDANT OR MERELY SIMILAR? COWBOY MUSIC IS JUST ONE AMONG THE MANY SOUNDS THAT GIVE COUNTRY MUSIC ITS VARIETY.

Cowboy music is as new as today's singing cowboys of the Grand Ole Opry, Riders In The Sky, and as old as Nathan Howard (Jack) Thorp, who published his *Songs Of The Cowboy* back in 1908. Cowboy music's earliest recordings, released in the mid Twenties, incorporated the flavor of what would later be referred to as western music.

The first singing cowboy was actor Ken Maynard. Maynard, who starred in the 1930 motion picture *The Wagon Master*, sang his Columbia recordings of 'The Lone-Star Trail' and 'Cowboy's Lament' in that film.

Certainly there were real-life singing cowboys nearly a century before, for cowpokes worked the range singing such traditional songs as 'The Old Chisholm Trail,' 'Sam Bass,' and 'Get Along Little Dogies.' Musical accompaniment on the trail was rare, however, save for an occasional fiddle or Jew's harp. With the domestication of the West, real cowboys disappeared, their legacy largely preserved by Hollywood imagery. For example, John Wayne was cast briefly as a singing cowboy until it became clear that he couldn't carry a tune.

the story of country

Roy Rogers, "King of the Cowboys," with Dale Evans and Trigger brought cowboy music to the TV generation.

One who could was a young WLS *National Barn Dance* performer and vaudeville veteran named Gene Autry. Never mind that Autry didn't care much for horses, he starred in over 90 Hollywood feature-length films (beginning with *Tumbling Tumbleweeds* in 1935, following a singing appearance in a Ken Maynard movie, I*n Old Santa Fe*, in 1934).

The host of CBS Radio's *Melody Ranch* for 17 years, Autry is famous for his renditions of 'Cowboy Yodel,' 'Don't Fence Me In' and 'Back in the Saddle Again.' 'Tumbling Tumbleweeds,' recorded by Autry, was a bigger hit for the Sons Of The Pioneers, first in 1934 and again in 1948.

Tex Ritter, "The Arizona Cowboy" Rex Allen, and "The King of the Cowboys" Roy Rogers, have perhaps surpassed Autry's contributions as singing cowboys. Many of Autry's biggest hits were of the order of 'Buttons And Bows' and his signature song, 'Rudolph The Red-Nosed Reindeer.'

A long list of other country singers who occasionally recorded cowboy songs includes Johnny Bond, Jimmy Wakely, Al Dexter, Merle Travis, Marty Robbins and Johnny Cash. *Johnny Cash Sings The Ballads Of The True West* includes such songs as 'Bury Me Not On The Lone Prairie' and 'The Streets Of Laredo.' Cash cut the themes from two American western TV series, *The Rebel Johnny Yuma* and *Bonanza* for his *Ring Of Fire* LP.

Patsy Montana is known worldwide for 'I Want To Be A Cowboy's Sweetheart,' while Patsy Cline recorded 'The Wayward Wind.' Even Eddy Arnold got in the act with his smash recording of 'Cattle Call,' followed by fellow Country Music Hall-of-Famer Hank Thompson, famous for his 1961 recording, 'Oklahoma Hills.' And the Statler Brothers paid homage to Gene Autry, Roy Rogers, Tex Ritter and others in their recording of 'What Ever Happened To Randolph Scott.'

Ed Bruce's hit, 'Mamas Don't Let Your Babies Grow Up to Be Cowboys' was released in 1976. Waylon (Jennings) And Willie (Nelson) covered Bruce's record and their version went to Number 1 on the *Billboard* charts 2 years later. Bruce had another hit with 'The Last Cowboy Song' in 1980.

Rex Allen, Jr, a modern-day preservationist of the cowboy music legacy, has recorded tribute songs ranging from 'Can You Hear Those Pioneers' to 'Last Of The Silver Screen Cowboys' (with Roy Rogers and Rex Allen, Sr).

Rex Allen, "The Arizona Cowboy," made the transition from movie cowboy to TV singing star in the Fifties.

Western TV series are no longer being produced and cowboy country endures largely thanks to the Warner Western label which, in 1992, released its first album, Don Edwards' *Songs Of The Trail* LP.

Another Warner Western act known as the Sons Of The San Joaquin claim the Sons Of The Pioneers as musical influences. The former's first album is titled *A Cowboy Has To Sing*. Cowboy poet Waddie Mitchell's début album for Warner Western is *Lone Driftin' Cowboy*. Riders In The Sky carry on the legacy of cowboy country, teaching today's children the ethic of living "the cowboy way." Ranger Doug writes the trio's material, yodels and acts as the Riders' master of ceremonies. Too Slim is the trio's lead singer and chief comedian, while Woody Paul plays guitar, harmonica and five-string banjo.

Garth Brooks sings of his worn-out Chris LeDoux tape, and the gold certification of LeDoux's *Whatcha' Gonna Do With A Cowboy* in 1993 underscores that there is still a demand for cowboy country music.

BLUEGRASS

The Brainchild of One Man

SOMETIMES THE TITLES "KING OF COUNTRY MUSIC" AND "QUEEN OF COUNTRY MUSIC" HAVE BEEN AWARDED TO ENTERTAINERS OTHER THAN THE ENTITLED DESIGNEES, ROY ACUFF AND KITTY WELLS. BUT THERE IS NO DISPUTING THAT THE "FATHER OF BLUEGRASS MUSIC" IS WILLIAM SMITH MONROE.

It has always been so, though Monroe's earliest pre-bluegrass performances were a uniquely American blend of string-band music, traditional hillbilly and Southern gospel influences.

Bluegrass music takes its name not from the state of Kentucky but from the name of Bill Monroe's band, the Blue Grass Boys, whose earliest Columbia Records recordings date back to 1946.

The music itself is one of American string-bands whose unique style is evidenced when they trade licks that back their high-pitched, nasal, often lonesome, tight vocal harmonies at breakneck speed. Rooted in the country music of the Thirties and Forties, bluegrass achieves its effects with acoustic instruments such as the fiddle, mandolin, five-string banjo, Dobro and guitar.

When Bill Monroe auditioned for the Grand Ole Opry in 1939, one of the tunes he chose was 'Mule Skinner Blues,' a Jimmie Rodgers and George Vaughn composition that has become a bluegrass music standard. Monroe's sidemen have included such disparate personalities as Milburn, New Jersey fiddler Gene Lowinger (introduced by Monroe as "the only Jewish bluegrass cowboy in the country"), Vassar Clements, Doug Green (who went on to greater fame as Riders In The Sky's "Ranger Doug") Kenny Baker, Byron Berline and Bill's bass-playing son, James.

One of the first Blue Grass Boys was Clyde Moody. Moody replaced guitarist Cleo Davis, who in later years would enjoy solo success with three hit records as "the Hillbilly Waltz King." During the early Forties, a fiddler named Howard "Howdy" Forrester (who went on to become one of Roy Acuff's Smoky Mountain Boys) and a five-string banjoist named David Akeman (known to *Hee Haw* viewers as the droll comedian Stringbean) joined the Blue Grass Boys. By 1945, the band also included guitar-playing singer/songwriter Lester Flatt.

Shortly after David Akeman left the Blue Grass Boys in September 1945, Monroe hired a 21-year-old North Carolina banjo player named Earl Scruggs. Scruggs had an unprecedented ability to play three-finger roll melody on the banjo and was the first musician to popularize the banjo as a lead instrument. (Before Scruggs appeared, the banjo was primarily used in comedy and novelty acts.) It was Earl's innovative three-finger picking technique mixed with Bill Monroe and Lester Flatt's quick-paced fiddle runs that produced the signature sound of Bill Monroe and the Blue Grass Boys.

By 1948 the Blue Grass Boys' leading lights, Lester Flatt and Earl Scruggs, had grown restless. Bill Monroe downplayed their departure from his band, dismissing it as normal band turnover, but it was an historic development in the history of bluegrass music.

A five-string banjoist named Don Reno joined the Blue Grass Boys following Earl Scruggs's departure. But a year later, in 1949, Reno left to form a duet with singer/guitarist Red Smiley. Meanwhile, Flatt and Scruggs teamed to form Lester Flatt, Earl Scruggs and (with a quintet of musicians, four of whom were former Blue Grass Boys) the Foggy Mountain Boys.

Flatt and Scruggs became a successful duo right from the start. After recording for Mercury Records from 1948 through 1950, Flatt and Scruggs signed with Columbia Records where five of their 20 chart records released between 1952 and 1968 became Top 10 hits. (The most famous of these, 'The Ballad of Jed Clampett,' was the theme song for the popular CBS TV series, *The Beverly Hillbillies*. The song was Flatt and Scruggs's only Number 1 country record, holding that position for 3 weeks.

Lester and Earl not only sang and played the theme music and provided snippets of instrumental music interspersed with the show's dialogue, they also made annual guest appearances. And further, they provided the theme music for two other CBS TV comedies, *Petticoat Junction* (1963–70) and *Green Acres* (1965–71).

Flatt and Scruggs's original 1949 recording of 'Foggy Mountain Breakdown' was adapted for the soundtrack of the 1967 movie *Bonnie and Clyde*. Capitalizing on the

movie's popularity, the Osborne Brothers, calling themselves the Bluegrass Banjo Pickers, recorded an LP with the cumbersome title of *Foggy Mountain Breakdown And Other Music From The Bonnie And Clyde Era*.

Ironically, despite their continuing achievements, Flatt and Scruggs split up in March, 1969. The break-up was precipitated by health difficulties, aggravated by competition in the shape of Earl's sons Gary and Randy, Earl Scruggs's flagging interest in traditional bluegrass and Flatt's refusal to perform the rock/folk-flavored bluegrass of the long-haired counterculture.

Lester Flatt went on to form the Nashville Grass, while Earl's sons joined their father as the Earl Scruggs Revue. Earl Scruggs was also one of a number of bluegrass artists who joined Roy Acuff and others on the Nitty Gritty Dirt Band's landmark album, *Will The Circle Be Unbroken*, recorded in 1972.

Also in the bluegrass tradition were the Stanley Brothers from Dickenson County, Virginia. Carter Stanley sang lead and played guitar alongside his brother, Ralph, who sang tenor and played banjo. They began their recording career in 1947, patterning their music after that of Bill Monroe, Lester Flatt and Earl Scruggs.

Carter, who MCed the Stanley Brothers' shows, and Ralph recorded the classic 'Molly and Tenbrooks' in 1948, but the following years were not lucrative and they disbanded briefly in 1951, Carter Stanley becoming one of the Blue Grass Boys. Subsequently, the Stanleys regrouped and in 1960 their recording of 'How Far To Little Rock' went to Number 17 on *Billboard*'s country chart.

Keith Whitley and Ricky Skaggs, who played in the East Kentucky Mountain Boys bluegrass band from 1968 through the early Seventies, were members of Ralph Stanley's Clinch Mountain Boys during the summer of 1970. They rejoined Stanley in 1971 through October 1972 and Keith became Ralph's lead singer in 1974.

At the same time that Flatt and Scruggs were enjoying their earliest

Former Blue Grass Boys Lester Flatt and Earl Scruggs brought bluegrass music to Sixties' American television.

success, Kentucky's Bobby and Sonny Osborne began to make their mark. Bobby had played mandolin with the Stanley Brothers before teaming with his five- and later six-string banjoist brother.

The Osborne Brothers performed on Knoxville, Tennessee's WROL Radio in 1953 and during the mid-Fifties they recorded with Jimmy Martin. (Martin, one of the Blue Grass Boys from 1949 to 1954, had a band called the Sunny Mountain Boys and had been a favorite on the WJR *Detroit Barn Dance* before moving on to the *Louisiana Hayride*

and then to the WWVA *Wheeling Jamboree* in 1956.)

The Osborne Brothers signed with MGM Records in 1956. The blend of Bobby's high lead vocal with Sonny's beautiful baritone brought them 16 charting singles between 1958 and 1976, including 'Roll Muddy River,' 'Rocky Top' (one of Tennessee's state songs), 'Ruby' (a bluegrass favorite subsequently covered by Buck Owens), 'Georgia Pineywoods' and 'Midnight Flyer.'

The Osborne Brothers' greatest recording success came when they signed with Decca Records (now MCA Records) in 1963, enhanced by induction into the Grand Ole Opry in August 1964. When the Osbornes left MCA for the independent CMH record label, they teamed with Mac Wiseman to record that perennial favorite, 'I Can Hear Kentucky Calling Me,' and a song called 'Shackles and Chains.'

Sonny Osborne's "single-string" banjo technique is a featured part of the Brothers' Opry act, as is Bobby's expertise as a "hoedown" fiddler. Bobby's pulsating, driving approach to the mandolin has also been dubbed "bluegrass jazz."

Brothers Jim and Jesse McReynolds, natives of Coeburn, Virginia, are another bluegrass act with a long association with the Grand Ole Opry, members since 1964. Jim is a tenor/guitarist. Jesse is best known for his "cross-picking" style of playing the mandolin. The brothers are backed by the Virginia Boys on fiddle and five-string banjo.

Jim and Jesse recorded for Capitol from 1952 through 1956. None of their songs was released until 1958, due to the advent of rock 'n' roll eclipsing all forms of country music. A Far Eastern tour resulted in the release of a two-record set titled *Jim And Jesse—Live In Japan*.

Malcolm "Mac" Wiseman, a Virginia-born banjoist/guitarist, worked briefly in 1949 as Bill Monroe's lead singer and guitarist. In 1950, he started his own group, known for its trademark twin harmony fiddles. From 1953 through 1956, Wiseman was a regular on Richmond, Virginia's WRVA *Old Dominion Barn Dance*.

Jim and Jesse McReynolds, Opry stars and world-wide ambassadors for bluegrass music.

Out of Lincolnton, Georgia, came the Lewis Family. One of the first famous bluegrass groups to feature female vocalists, the Lewis Family was also known for singing gospel music to the accompaniment of bluegrass-style instrumentation.

Bluegrass music was a favorite among the college crowd all across America, long before today's country music began to find favor with them. On college campuses around the Washington, DC, area artists like Emmylou Harris, Jimmy Dean, Roy

Clark, the Country Gentlemen and the Seldom Scene were regional institutions before attaining national and international prominence.

The Country Gentlemen formed in 1957, recorded for Starday Records and had a strong urban bluegrass following. It was the Country Gentlemen's recording of 'The Long Black Veil' that inspired cover recordings by the Kingston Trio and Joan Baez of the Lefty Frizzell classic. (In his late teens, Ricky Skaggs briefly played fiddle for the Country Gentlemen before forming his own band, Boone Creek, in 1977.)

On America's west coast, the earliest members of a southern California bluegrass band known as the Golden State Boys renamed themselves the Hillmen in 1963. Among the Hillmen were brothers Vern and Rex Gosdin, who later recorded as the Gosdin Brothers. Their 1967 hit 'Hangin' On' was subsequently released as a solo by Vern in 1976. They have since established careers as solo artists.

Another Hillmen alumnus is a former member of the Scottsville

Squirrel Barkers, a California mandolinist named Chris Hillman. Hillman went on to greater fame as one of the Byrds from 1964 through 1968. In 1968, he formed yet another group, the Flying Burrito Brothers with Gram Parsons. Following Parsons' death, Hillman developed a solo career from 1972 through 1986 when he became a member of the Desert Rose Band.

During the mid Sixties the first bluegrass festivals were held in and around Virginia. By 1967 Bill Monroe had established his own in Beam Blossom, Indiana, which continues to this day.

The Dillards, Doug and Rodney, are credited with popularizing bluegrass among folk music fans. Their albums brought fiddle music a younger, hipper audience who also enjoyed the Dillards' electrified bluegrass form of country rock.

The Dillards recorded an early (1963) version of 'Dueling Banjos' (titled 'Mocking Banjos' when Carl Story with the Brewster Brothers recorded it in 1957). Written as 'Feuding Banjos,' and originally

Bill Monroe, "the Father of Bluegrass Music." In the eyes of purists, he *is* bluegrass music.

recorded in 1955 by Don Reno and Arthur "Guitar Boogie" Smith, the song was retitled 'Dueling Banjos,' recorded by session musicians Eric Weissberg and Steve Mandell, and featured on the soundtrack of the 1972 movie *Deliverance*.

Coinciding with the release of *Deliverance*, four members of a group called the Bluegrass Alliance formed New Grass Revival, a name given the quartet by its mandolin and fiddle player, Sam Bush. Bush (who as a teenager won a fiddling contest in

1968 and again in 1969) and his group infused rock music into their bluegrass. The electric pick-ups they used gave their acoustic instruments greater volume. In its last incarnation, the New Grass Revival consisted of Sam Bush, John Cowan, Bela Fleck and Pat Flynn. The group had four charted releases between 1986 and 1988. The New Grass Revival disbanded, following one of their most popular records titled, ironically, 'Can't Stop Now.'

Ricky Skaggs, a contemporary of New Grass Revival, exemplifies the continuation of the bluegrass tradition. While giving the music a modern sound, Skaggs's musical inspiration comes not only from original material but Ricky's versions of old Flatt and Scruggs numbers from the Fifties, which made songs such as 'Crying My Heart Out Over You' and 'Don't Get Above Your Raisin'' hits once again.

Entertainers such as Skaggs, the Whites, and newcomer Alison Krauss and Union Station, are assuring the continued popularity of bluegrass music through the Nineties.

COUNTRY GOSPEL

Praise The Lord—
Country Style

COUNTRY MUSIC HAS A STRONG FOUNDATION IN THE RELIGIOUS HERITAGE OF CHRISTIAN—MORE SPECIFICALLY WHITE PROTESTANT—AMERICA. MOST COUNTRY ARTISTS HAVE RECORDED AT LEAST ONE ALBUM OF SACRED SONGS; INDEED IT IS ALMOST EXPECTED.

Traditionally, country music artists have received their earliest encouragement from singing in church as children. Depending upon the denomination, a country star's earliest memories are of hymns or more fervent gospel songs.

Hymns met the needs of American's European ancestry. Their descendants, increasingly of an evangelistic bent, were less interested in songs of glorification than in saving the souls of backsliding Christians and "non-believers." Christian fundamentalists of whatever hue can be credited with the popularity of the country-flavored sacred music that endures today.

The Carter Family were among the first popular country musicians to prove the appeal of the gospel sound. In 1928 they recorded 'Keep On The Sunny Side Of Life' and their 1935 recording of 'Can the Circle Be Unbroken' was responsible for interest in the composition some 37 years later by the Nitty Gritty Dirt Band. The Dirt Band recorded the song first in 1972 and then again in 1989. Also, traveling gospel quartets of the Thirties, such as the Swanee River Boys, were sponsored by religious song publishers to increase sales of their copyrighted material.

Among the Gospel-inspired songs to find a permanent place in country music are Albert Brumley's 1932 standard 'I'll Fly Away,' and 'Turn Your Radio On' (recorded by Ray Stevens in 1972 and again by the Statler Brothers 20 years later), Roy Acuff's 'Great Speckled Bird,' Eddy Arnold's version of 'May The Good Lord Bless And Keep You' and 'I Saw The Light,' written in 1948 and still a favorite. The most famous though is undoubtedly 'Amazing Grace.' Never a commercial hit as a country song (Judy Collins' 1970 rendition remains the definitive pop hit), it was recorded as early as 1926 and remains a staple in the repertoire of many country artists, from the Statler Brothers to the Nitty Gritty Dirt Band. Even Buck Owens acknowledges the song in the title of his 1973 hit, 'Ain't It Amazin' Gracie.'

Country gospel fervor was quite apparent in the Fifties. Red Foley followed 'Just A Closer Walk With Thee' (covered by Patsy Cline) in 1951 with '(There Will Be) Peace In The Valley (For Me),' the first million-selling gospel song. Stuart Hamblen wrote 'It Is No Secret (What G-d Can Do)' in 1950. When he released his recording of the song the following year, it was a Top 10 record. Martha Carson rallied from the pain of divorce to write the country gospel handclapper 'Satisfied' as an affirmation of hope and religious faith. Carson's recording of 'Satisfied' was released in 1951. Ferlin Husky's 'Wings Of A Dove' gave him a Number 1 country record in 1960 and won such widespread acceptance that it reached Number 12 on *Billboard*'s pop music chart.

The Browns' adaptation of an old song of inspiration, 'The Three Bells,' sold over one million copies in 1959 and was the first song ever to attain the Number 1 position on the country, pop and rhythm and blues (R&B) charts.

Country songs with spiritual themes continued to be popular during the Sixties. Bill Anderson's 1962 recording 'Mama Sang A Song' was not only a tribute to "Mama," it incorporated the refrain "What a

Martha Carson: her signature song was country gospel handclapper 'Satisfied.'

friend we have in Jesus." Not surprisingly, it was a Number 1 hit.

Johnny Cash had a Number 1 record on Carl Perkins' 'Daddy Sang Bass' in 1968. He has often included religious material on secular country albums, such as 'Were You There' (from *Ring Of Fire*), 'These Hands' and the recitation 'Here Was A Man' (*The Johnny Cash Show*). 'Jesus Was A Carpenter'

appears on the LP *Hello, I'm Johnny Cash*.

Glen Campbell alluded to biblical instruction in both his 1968 duet with Bobbie Gentry, 'A Little Less Of Me' and in his 1969 admonition, 'Try A Little Kindness.' The following year Campbell covered the Edwin Hawkins' Singers' 1969 spiritual 'Oh Happy Day.'

Jeannie C. Riley's 'Oh, Singer' went to Number 4 in *Billboard* in 1971 and crossed over to the pop charts. That same year songwriter Harlan Howard recorded 'Sunday Morning Christian.' Tom T. Hall recorded 'Me And Jesus' with the Mount Pisgah United Methodist Church Choir in 1972. A gospel-flavored duet was also big that year: 'Let's All Go Down To The River,' recorded by Jody Miller and Johnny Paycheck.

Kris Kristofferson's gold recording of 'Why Me' reached Number 1 on the country charts and Number 16 on the pop charts in 1973. That same year Glen Campbell made both the country and pop charts with 'I Knew Jesus (Before He Was A Superstar).' Elvis Presley (in 1974) and Ray Price (in 1977) had country hits with the Larry Gatlin composition, 'Help Me.' Bobby Bare surprised country listeners with his recording of Paul Craft's irreverent 'Drop Kick Me Jesus' in 1976. Craft recorded 'Lean On Jesus (Before He Leans On You)' in 1977.

The Statler Brothers' recording of 'How Great Thou Art' (a nineteenth century Swedish poem) reached Number 39 on *Billboard*'s country chart in 1976. The spiritual reappears on the Statlers' TV album along with such favorites as 'Love Lifted Me,' 'Have A Little Talk With Jesus,' 'The Old Rugged Cross' and a song that dates back to 1899, 'When The Roll Is Called Up Yonder.'

Tom T. Hall was back in 1977 with his 'May The Force Be With You Always' (also a play-on-words

tribute to the movie *Star Wars*). Kristofferson's 'They Killed Him' (a tribute to Jesus, Gandhi and Martin Luther King, Jr) made both the pop and country charts in 1987. Also in 1987, Ray Stevens took a poke at TV evangelists with 'Would Jesus Wear A Rolex?' In 1992 Confederate Railroad had a hit with 'Jesus And Momma.'

Drugs and alcohol figure in some of the more offbeat country songs with religious themes. The effects of a Saturday night hangover amid the

Country-gospel star Stuart Hamblen ran for President in 1952 on the Prohibition Party ticket.

ringing of a church bell are chronicled in Kris Kristofferson's composition, 'Sunday Mornin' Comin' Down.' Kristofferson, Ray Stevens and Ray Price are among the artists who have recorded 'Sunday Mornin' Comin' Down,' but it was Johnny Cash who had a Number 1 record with the song in 1969. 'Sam Stone,' recorded by John Prine in 1971, supposes that because of such evils as drug addiction, Jesus' death may have been in vain. Cal Smith's 1973 Number 1 hit of Bill Anderson's composition, 'The Lord Knows I'm Drinkin'' told the self-righteous to mind their own business.

Sacred music continues its popularity among country artists during the Nineties. Grand Ole Opry star Jack Greene has retitled his 1967 country smash, 'There Goes My Everything' and given it an evangelical slant as 'He Is My Everything.' The Friday Night Opry wouldn't be the same to many if its finale was not a segue into WSM Radio's *Grand Ole Gospel Time*, hosted by the Reverend Jimmie Snow (Hank Snow's son.)

ROCKABILLY

The Sun Sounds of Segregationist America

ROCKABILLY COMBINES THE ELEMENTS OF HILLBILLY MUSIC WITH THOSE OF PRIMITIVE ROCK 'N' ROLL. ROCKABILLY BEGAN IN RACIALLY SEGREGATED AMERICA AS THE MUSIC OF YOUNG, WHITE SOUTHERNERS WHO HAD AN APPRECIATION FOR THE MUSIC'S CONGLOMERATION OF TRADITIONAL COUNTRY, THE RHYTHMS OF EMERGING ROCK, AND THE BEAT OF "RACE" MUSIC.

These youngsters were searching for something beyond the smooth sounds of the popular music of the day. Not since Frank Sinatra, with his legion of bobby-soxer fans, had American young people had a music to call their own. Bill Haley And The Comets' 1955 release, 'Rock Around The Clock' filled the bill. Generally acknowledged as the first nationally popular rock 'n' roll hit, it was a hit again in 1974 when it re-emerged as the theme for the American Fifties-based TV sitcom *Happy Days*.

If Elvis Presley was the "King of Rock 'n' Roll," Bill Haley was its father. But Haley's signature song, along with his earlier recordings such as 'Crazy Man, Crazy' and 'Shake, Rattle And Roll,' suggest that his repertoire was more jazz- and less rural-influenced than that of Elvis Presley and Presley's rockabilly contemporaries. (Not that Haley couldn't claim country credentials: formerly a singing yodeler for a group called the Downhomers, he formed a band called the Four Aces Of Western Swing; out of which came the Saddlemen in 1949 and the Comets in 1953). Further, Haley's clean-cut image and lack of youth (real success eluded him until he was 30 years old) were not attributes to produce frenzied excitement in record-buying teenagers, who saved their screams for rockabilly's earliest teenaged idols.

Crooners, such as Pat Boone, had the boyish good looks but lacked the style. Boone's covers of Fats Domino's 'Ain't That A Shame' and Little Richard's 'Tutti Frutti' and 'Long Tall Sally,' made the music of black artists acceptable to white audiences—thereby giving rise to the unfair dismissal of Boone's creations as rip-offs of Fifties race music—but he lacked their soul.

George Jones, whose country music career was going nowhere in 1954, had the talent, but lacked the commitment to rockabilly. Jones, whose rockabilly recordings credited either the stage name "Thumper Jones" or "Hank Smith" as the artist, was just biding his time till he came out with the anything but stone country 'Why Baby Why,' taking it

Bill Haley And The Comets: the earliest and among the most countryfied of rockabilly acts.
....

to the top of the country charts. It's hard to imagine either Boone or Jones credibly exciting America's teenage girls in 1955 the way Elvis Presley did with the release of his début hit, 'Baby, Let's Play House.'

Bill Haley's string of moderately popular releases continued until 1960 (generally acknowledged as the end of rockabilly's heyday), but the torch had already been passed to Elvis Presley and Ricky Nelson.

In March 1957, less than 2 months short of his seventeenth birthday, Ricky Nelson covered Fats Domino's 'I'm Walkin'.' Débuting it on his family's TV series, *The Adventures of Ozzie and Harriet*, Ricky became an overnight singing sensation, selling over one million copies within a week.

Unlike Pat Boone, Nelson did not cover the work of more convincing black artists with his later rockabilly hits 'Stood Up,' 'My Bucket's Got A Hole In It' and 'Believe What You Say.' Rather, Nelson professed to be influenced by Elvis Presley and, when interviewed, indicated that one of his earliest idols was Carl Perkins.

Perkins, like many of the genuine rockabilly artists, recorded for the same label: Memphis, Tennessee-based Sun Records. Most music fans know the story of how Sun Records' owner and president Sam Phillips had been searching for a white youth who could sing like a black man. Coincidentally, the ideal candidate came to Sun. Elvis Presley walked into Sun studios to make a record of 'That's All Right, Mama,' for his mother, Gladys, paid his $4 and walked out. It took some doing, but once Presley's recording was brought to Phillips' attention the record executive tracked down the future King of Rock 'n' Roll and signed him up.

But Sun would not be a "one-artist" label, and among the other potential talents knocking on Phillips' door was Tennessean Carl Perkins.

Toward the end of 1955 Perkins took a true story he had heard about a young man's blue suede shoes, wrote a song about it and brought it to Sun studios in the hope of recording it. Phillips enjoyed Perkins' recording of 'Blue Suede Shoes' so much that he released it in January 1956. There was another consideration: RCA Records had just purchased Presley's contract from Sam Phillips. But Phillips believed that, in Perkins, he had a recording artist with a marketable style similar to that of Presley. Perkins followed up the success of 'Blue Suede Shoes' with such hits as 'Boppin' The Blues' and 'Dixie Fried' and 'Your True Love.'

Perkins' road to sustained success as a rockabilly artist met a detour on March 21, 1956 when he was seriously injured in an automobile accident. Several months of recuperation followed before he was able to resume his career, cutting short any momentum he had generated as a rockabilly artist. Like Elvis Presley before him, Perkins' stay at Sun Records was a short one. Perkins

Elvis Presley, Jerry Lee Lewis, Carl Perkins (on crutches) and Johnny Cash.

moved on to Columbia where his next releases would be 'Pink Pedal Pushers' and 'Pointed Toe Shoes.'

These early releases made both the country and pop charts, but his greatest success would come when his musical legacy was realized by the Beatles. The Fab Four recorded 'Matchbox,' 'Honey Don't' and 'Everybody's Trying To Be My Baby,' all songs from the pen of Carl Perkins. Perkins also toured as a part of Johnny Cash's road ensemble from 1965 through 1975. Today, with a string of moderately successful country songs to his credit, he proclaims himself to be cured from a recent bout of throat cancer.

Perkins' colleague, Johnny Cash, was another of the early Sun rockabilly artists. Like Perkins, Cash left Sun for Columbia. But before he did, in the years 1955–8, he turned out a string of hits: 'Cry, Cry, Cry,' 'Folsom Prison Blues,' 'I Walk The Line,' 'Get Rhythm,' 'There You Go,' 'Train Of Love,' 'Next In Line,' 'Don't Make Me Go,' 'Home Of The Blues,' 'Ballad Of A Teenage Queen,' 'Big River,' 'Guess Things Happen That Way,' 'The Ways Of A Woman In Love' and 'You're The Nearest Thing To Heaven.'

Cash continued to have hits for Sun once he signed with Columbia, since, beginning in 1959, Phillips decided to release songs he had "in the can" at Sun. 'Luther Played The Boogie' was the first such release, but Sun reissued 'Get Rhythm,' in 1969, released Cash's cover of Lonnie Donegan's 1956 hit 'Rock Island Line' in 1970, and reissued 'Big River,' also in 1970.

In January 1957 Elmo Lewis brought his son, Jerry Lee, a young

Ricky Nelson, with the Four Preps, brought wholesomeness and commitment to rockabilly music.

singing, honky-tonkin' pumpin' piano player just out of his teens, to audition for Sam and Judd Phillips. Four months laters Lewis recorded his first Sun single, 'Whole Lotta Shakin' Goin' On.' Both a pop and country smash, it was followed the next year with the biggest hit of Lewis's career, 'Great Balls of Fire.'

Jerry's December, 1957 release for Sun, the soulful 'You Win Again,' was followed in 1958 by releases that were more in the rockabilly vein: 'Breathless' and 'High School Confidential.' These records were the last major hits for "The Killer" until he rebounded in the late Sixties as a country singer following the listening public's collective amnesia concerning the scandal of his mar-

riage to his 13-year-old cousin, which had torpedoed his career.

Sun Records is a historical footnote in Charlie Rich's musical career. Rich, who hails from Colt, Arkansas, moved to Memphis to pursue his career. Once in the Bluff City, Rich cut an audition tape at Sun Records. Sam Phillips and Phillips' A&R director Bill Justis liked what they heard and signed Rich. But Charlie's attempts to launch a recording career at Sun were unsuccessful and he ended up doing mostly session work there.

His first taste of success came after he moved from Sun, in 1960 with 'Lonely Weekends.' "The Silver Fox", as the greying Rich came to be known, was next heard from in 1965 when he had a big hit with 'Mohair Sam.'

The Seventies were Charlie's most prolific years as he dominated the charts with a string of hits including 'Behind Closed Doors,' 'The Most Beautiful Girl,' 'There Won't Be Anymore,' 'A Very Special Love Song' and 'I Don't See Me In Your Eyes.'

Roy Orbison owed his Sun-launched career to his college buddy, Pat Boone. For it was Boone who, like Orbison, a student at North Texas State University, encouraged Roy to pursue a music career. It actually began on a smaller label, but it was at Sun that Orbison achieved his first hit, 'Ooby Dooby' in 1956.

Roy Orbison's later career was sustained by hits on the Monument, MGM, Warner and Virgin record labels, but his Sun days are historically relevant for reasons other than his success with 'Ooby Dooby.' For Orbison got a chance to gather around the piano at Sun's famous studio at 706 Union Street in Memphis and jam with labelmates Johnny Cash, Jerry Lee Lewis and Carl

Charlie Rich closed out the rockabilly era but was still recording in the Seventies.

Perkins. Unedited recordings from those informal Fifties' sessions were made. They were subsequently filed and forgotten until years later when a photo of what would be dubbed "The Million Dollar Quartet" surfaced along with the recordings. New interest in the rockabilly careers of Cash, Lewis, Orbison and Perkins during the 1980s gave rise to a musical reunion of this "quartet" of artists who, for purposes of that brief interlude, called themselves "The Class of '55."

The closest thing to that latter-day resurgence of interest in pure rockabilly occurred in 1982 in England. There, a group of American expatriates called the Stray Cats made waves among British fans (and later also among their own countrymen) with original songs (such as 'Rock This Town') inspired by Eddie Cochran, Gene Vincent and other earlier rockabillies.

Today, to stretch a point, it might be said that what strains of rockabilly remain have been incorporated into that loosely defined music known as country rock.

COUNTRY COMEDY and NOVELTY SONGS

Country Humor In Contemporary Song

WHEN DISCUSSING COUNTRY MUSIC'S COMEDY AND NOVELTY SONGS, SOME MUSICOLOGISTS LUMP THE TWO TOGETHER. IT IS SOMETIMES HARD TO TELL WHERE ONE CATEGORY LEAVES OFF AND THE OTHER BEGINS, FOR MOST NOVELTY SONGS ARE ALSO FUNNY. AND SINCE, UNLIKE OTHER FORMS OF MUSIC, COMIC SONGS TEND TO WEAR THIN AFTER A LISTENING OR TWO, MOST ARE DEFINITELY A NOVELTY.

Yet there is a difference between country's comedy and the genre's novelty songs. All that is required of a comic ditty is that it be funny (its country oriented references can be interchangable with others or even, in some cases, be entirely absent; its country credentials thinly existing because it is recorded by a country music star.)

A novelty song, on the other hand, to be popular, must also be at least marginally humorous, but it is more event-driven. And its popularity is generally as short-lived as interest in the event itself. Therefore, country's novelty tunes generally tend to have a considerably shorter "shelf life" than their comic counterparts.

Uncle Dave Macon—"the Dixie Dewdrop"—entertained Opry audiences for a quarter-century.

There's a close historical link between the more serious country music and its country cousin, comedy. The rural regions of the southern and south-eastern United States were the scenes of social occasions such as the house party and barn dance where neighbors traded funny stories and funny songs. It was in that atmosphere where one could hear a whimsical fiddle tune, or see a minstrel or medicine show that country's comic songs found their first audiences.

Uncle Dave Macon, a Grand Ole Opry star from the Opry's 1925 inception, was one of country music's earliest comedy singer/songwriters. Macon, known by several monickers including the "Joyful Minstrel of the Tennessee Hills," accompanied himself on the banjo, which he would flip and then swing as he sang such songs as 'Keep My Skillet Good And Greasy,' 'Chewing Gum,' and 'Carve That Possum.'

Uncle Dave, who had audiences laughing at his stage antics virtually right up until the time he died in 1952, lived long enough to chuckle at the comedy of his fellow Opry stars including comediennes Sarie and Sally and Cousin Minnie Pearl, as well as the humor of Archie Campbell, the Duke of Paducah and a host of others. Listening to his radio in 1944, Uncle Dave might have heard the Hoosier Hot Shots' rendition of 'She Broke My Heart In Three Places.'

In 1945, with the war years drawing to a close, "The Kansas Jayhawk," Carson Robison, sang 'Hitler's Last Letter To Hirohito'.

(Robison followed that Number 5 record with a lighter composition, which peaked on the country charts at Number 3, titled 'Life Gets Tee-Jus Don't It.') In 1946, Bill Carlisle had a hit with the first of a series of novelty songs which he and his group, the Carlisles, still perform on the Grand Ole Opry today. 'Rainbow At Midnight' was followed by 'What Kinda Deal Is This,' 'No Help Wanted,' 'Is Zat You, Myrtle' and others. In 1948 listeners were guffawing at a tune that would certainly be politically incorrect by Nineties' standards: Esmereldy's 'Slap Her Down Again, Paw.'

That same year, record buyers were wearing out the vinyl as they scratched their heads trying to fol-

Homer And Jethro: Homer Haynes (guitar) and Jethro Burns (mandolin) popularized parodies of country hits.

low the progression of Lonzo and Oscar's classic 'I'm My Own Grandpaw.' In 1950 Cactus Pryor And The Pricklypears (sic) had a Top 10 hit with the novelty number 'Cry Of The Dying Duck In A Thunderstorm.'

Also during the Fifties, Ferlin Husky decided country music needed a comic philosopher, so Husky invented one in the person of his alter ego, Simon Crumb. "Crumb" had two Top 5 novelty hits: 'Cuzz You're So Sweet' (1955) and 'Country Music Is Here To Stay' (1958). While country audiences know "Crumb"—the character has remained in Husky's live performances down through the years, thanks, in part, to television—even Americans who didn't keep up with country music were aware of Homer and Jethro.

Henry D. "Homer" Haynes and Kenneth C. "Jethro" Burns became a musical comedy duo in 1932, working the country fair circuit and local radio shows including Knoxville, Tennessee's *Mid-Day Merry-Go-Round*.

With Homer on guitar and Jethro (who was Chet Atkins's brother-in-law) on mandolin, the comedy team received even greater recognition when, in 1950, they began a 10-year run as regulars on Chicago's WLS *National Barn Dance*.

Their credits during the *National Barn Dance* years included appearances on the Grand Ole Opry and Jimmy Dean's television show; this on the strength of a recording career that began in 1949 with the release of Homer and Jethro's first novelty song, 'I Feel That Old Age Comin' On.' That same year the duo had an even bigger record with one of the great country comediennes of the day, June Carter.

By 1953, Homer And Jethro were recording the kinds of songs which would become their trademark: parodies. Their first, a take-off of Patti Page's 'The Doggie In The Window,' was '(How Much Is That) Hound Dog In The Window.' Homer And Jethro spoofed Jimmie Rodgers' 'In The

Johnny Bond—the country musician who scored several hits with his unique satires on drunkenness.

Jailhouse Now,' and Skeets McDonald's 'Don't Let The Stars Get In Your Eyes' with their 'I'm In The Jailhouse Now' and 'Don't Let The Stars Get In Your Eyeballs.' Titles of Homer And Jethro's albums were equally creative: these include *The Worst Of Homer And Jethro*, *Songs My Mother Never Sang* and *Homer And Jethro Strike Back*.

A couple of years after they left the *National Barn Dance* in 1960, Homer And Jethro became the commercial spokespersons for Kellogg's Corn Flakes, sponsors of the *Beverly Hillbillies*, endearing themselves to fans of the TV series with what became Homer And Jethro's trademark slogan: "Ooh, that's corny!" (A Homer And Jethro album bears that title.)

Homer And Jethro remained popular until Haynes's death in 1971. In 1976, Burns found a "new" Homer, a 28-year-old school teacher named Ken Eidson, but the new team didn't share the mass popularity of the old, and by the time of Burns's death in 1989, it was apparent that the magic of the original Homer And Jethro just couldn't be duplicated.

But Homer And Jethro's legacy was not lost on their contemporaries, nor on country's comic talents which succeeded them. Back in 1961, Don Reno and Red Smiley, calling themselves Chick And His Hot Rods, chided Opry stars Little Jimmy Dickens and Ernest Tubb with a ditty called 'Jimmy Caught The Dickens (Pushing Ernest In The Tub).' Also in 1961, Jim Nesbitt, the "'Lasses Sopper," began his 10-year string of country novelty releases with a plea to the then president, 'Please Mr Kennedy,' to the tune of the American classic, 'The Ballad of Davy Crockett.'

Two years later, velvet-voiced Opry star Roy Drusky broke with his image to record the novelty hit, 'Peel Me A Nanner,' about a man whose significant other made a monkey out of him. Don Bowman recorded a string of novelty numbers during the Sixties, the most popular of which was his 1964 ode to Chet Atkins called 'Chit Atkins, Make Me A Star.' And in 1969 even Mac Wiseman got into the act with his tale of 'Johnny's Cash And Charley's Pride.'

The Geesinslaw Brothers, Sam (Alldred) and Son (DeWayne Smith), recorded several novelty songs in the Sixties, including a 1967 parody of Kenny Rogers' 'Ruby, Don't Take Your Love To Town,' called 'Chubby, Please Take Your Love To Town.' (The Geesinslaws' penchant for parody continues into the Nineties. In 1992, a television commercial featuring an elderly lady in distress crying out 'I've Fallen And I Can't Get Up,' prompted the Geesinslaws to record Clinton Gregory's 'I'm White And I Can't Get Down.')

If innocence was on its way out in the Sixties, the times had not yet become too profound to laugh about that staple of many a country song: drinking. From the Forties until the time of his death from a heart attack in 1978, Johnny Bond satirized drunkenness in several of his country songs. One of the most popular was '10 Little Bottles.' First released in the Forties, '10 Little Bottles' became an even bigger hit for Bond in 1965.

Sheb Wooley's alter ego, Ben Colder, who got laughs with his parodies of Rex Allen's 'Don't Go Near The Indians,' Willie Nelson's 'Hello

Walls' and David Houston's 'Almost Persuaded' (reprised as 'Don't Go Near The Eskimos,' 'Hello Wall No. 2' and 'Almost Persuaded No. 2') during the Sixties, returned in 1971 with his take on Conway Twitty's 'Fifteen Years Ago,' titled 'Fifteen Beers Ago.'

And, to this day, Don Bowman (once a part of the Bill Anderson show) gets laughs with his adaptation of Anderson's heart-rending 'Still.' Bowman perverts Bill's intent of loving "you still" to "your still". (Anderson's own alliterative novelty number, 'Double S,' a 1978 release, was spoofed by an artist calling himself Whisperin' Will and his 1979 release, 'Double W'.) Jerry Clower, a country humorist who was formerly a fertilizer salesman in Yazoo, Mississippi, has sold millions of recordings since the early Seventies with his riotous tales of southern life.

Johnny Cash, who recorded an album of novelty songs (*Everybody Loves A Nut*) prior to his biggest novelty hit, 'A Boy Named Sue,' in 1969, was the subject of two novelty songs in 1970 (Jane Morgan's "answer" recording of 'A Girl Named Johnny Cash,' and Cash associate Gordon Terry's 'The Ballad of Johnny Cash'), and another in 1973: Onie Wheeler's 'John's Been Shuckin' My Corn,' recorded in response to Cash's 1972 esoteric jibe titled 'Oney' (sic).

Also in 1972, Roy Clark brought out 'The Lawrence Welk-Hee Haw Counter-Revolution Polks.' Jim Stafford's string of Seventies novelty numbers included 'My Girl Bill' and 'Wildwood Weed.' Dick Feller also climbed the charts during the early Seventies with his novelty hits, 'Biff, The Friendly Purple Bear,' 'Makin' The Best Of A Bad Situation,' and 'The Credit Card Song.'

If citizens band radios were the rage of Seventies America, then C. W. McCall ('Convoy') and Cledus Maggard ('The White Knight') were the best known of all the artists suddenly recording CB songs. By 1979, such subjects as America's gas shortage and international terrorism became the inspiration for novelty songs such as Bobby Butler's 'Cheaper Crude or No More Food,' and Roger Hallmark and the Thrasher Brothers' 'A Message To Khoumeini.'

In 1980, Bobby Bare poked fun at the sexist practice of numerically rating members of the opposite gender with his recording of 'Numbers.' In 1984, Moe Bandy and Joe Stampley parodied Boy George's music with their hit, 'Where's The Dress.' And well in time for Christmas, 1984, Elmo 'n' Patsy released their perennial yuletide novelty classic, 'Grandma Got Run Over By A Reindeer.'

Any discussion of country's comedy and novelty songs would be incomplete without the mention of Ray Stevens. Stevens, who has made a career of recording novelty songs (since 1961 on the pop charts), had his first novelty hit on the country charts in 1974 with 'The Streak.' Since then, Stevens has got laughs from country listeners with his bluegrass version of the Johnny Mathis standard 'Misty' (1975) and such hits as 'Shriner's Convention' (1980) and

'Mississippi Squirrel Revival' (1984). In 1977, recording under the name Henhouse Five Plus Two, Stevens parodied a bunch of chickens pecking out the famous Glenn Miller instrumental 'In The Mood.'

The duo of (Sandy) Pinkard and (Richard) Bowden, who have recorded country parodies since 1984, remind many of a modern-day Homer And Jethro.

With songs such as 'Drivin' My Wife Away' (a parody of Eddie Rabbitt's 'Drivin' My Life Away'), 'Mama, She's Lazy,' (a "tribute" to the Judds' 'Mama, He's Crazy') and 'She Thinks I Steal Cars' (a broad rewrite of the George Jones hit, 'She Thinks I Still Care), Pinkard And Bowden play to audiences too young to remember Homer And Jethro—as well as to those who do—assuring the continued popularity of country's novelty and comedy songs in the Nineties.

Ray Stevens' novelty songs have made him a favorite with country fans.

COUNTRY DANCE

High Steppin' Country

IF DANCING CAN BE TRACED BACK TO WHEN OUR ANCESTORS FIRST STOOD UPRIGHT, THEN COUNTRY DANCING CAN BE SAID TO HAVE THE SAME ORIGIN AS THE MUSIC. REFERENCES HAVE ALREADY BEEN MADE TO THE JIGS AND REELS OF YESTERYEAR. IT IS ALSO KNOWN THAT SQUARE DANCING BECAME A POPULAR FORM OF RHYTHMIC AMUSEMENT AROUND 1865.

In 1980 Tennessee's state legislature recognized Appalachian square dancing—a form of dance associated with the middle Tennessee area, including Nashville—designating it as Tennessee's official state dance.

Similarly, clogging, a form of dance involving the wearing of heavy shoes that hammer out the beat, goes back to the 1880s. The high-stepping dance was brought over to America by Irish, German and Dutch immigrants, many of whom settled in western North Carolina.

Texans are likely to have danced some variation of the Texas Two-Step as long as there has been a Lone Star state, and back in 1925, the time of the Grand Ole Opry's inception, Uncle Dave Macon's act included a buck dancer named Dancing Bob Bradford. During the Thirties, the Colby Agricultural Square Dancers (also called the Fred Colby Square Dancers) became Opry regulars, remaining until 1945 when the Cedar Hill Dancers began their 10-year stint with the radio stage show.

Country dance, in fact, remains an Opry staple, preserved largely through the assistance of the Opry's Melvin Sloan Dancers and the Stoney Mountain Cloggers. In 1952, a group of Appalachian-style square dancers led by Ralph Sloan were invited to join the Grand Ole Opry. Sloan's group, the Tennessee Travelers, were well known and respected for their special form of high-energy foot-stomping and hand-clapping throughout Ralph's 28 years with the Opry. When Sloan died in 1980, his brother Melvin stepped in, carrying on the tradition as one of eight hoofers who now call themselves the Melvin Sloan Dancers.

As both the Tennessee Travelers and the Melvin Sloan Dancers, this four-couple dance troupe has been featured at the Opry and widely on television. In 1983, at President Reagan's request, the Melvin Sloan Dancers performed at Washington, DC's famed John F. Kennedy Center in a salute to Roy Acuff. Melvin Sloan was honored again in 1990 when his stage costume and dancing shoes were donated to the

Country Music Foundation's Hall of Fame at a special presentation.

A second group of Opry square dancers is much in evidence in the form of the Stoney Mountain Cloggers, a dance troupe of six with fans numbering in the millions. Originally billed as Ben Smathers and the Stoney Mountain Cloggers, Ben and Margaret Smathers and their children were frequent entrants in dance contests, becoming so popular that they were invited to appear regularly on TV shows in Greenville and Asheville, North Carolina.

By the late Fifties their regional fame had come to the attention of Grand Ole Opry officials who invited the cloggers to do a guest spot. Repeated ovations and encores resulted in a formal invitation to join the Opry that same year.

During the Seventies, Ben Smathers and the Stoney Mountain Cloggers were named "Dance Masters of Country Music." Ben Smathers also received the Country Music Association's President's Award, in recognition of his contribution to country music.

Known for a clogging style which he described as a mixture of tap, jitterbug and square dancing, Ben Smathers taught these steps to his family, much as they had been taught to him as a child by an octegenarian friend of the family.

In 1990 the Opry was dealt another blow with the passing of Ben Smathers. But Smathers' family honors his memory with their every Opry performance as they continue, now billed as the Stoney Mountain Cloggers, to carry on the tradition.

Louise Mandrell, once a recording artist like her sister, Barbara, is an accomplished dancer who has thrilled audiences all over the United States, particularly in Las Vegas and in her acclaimed stage show at Nashville's Opryland theme park.

Mandrell's choreographer is Melanie Greenwood, a former Las Vegas dancer and host of *Dancin' USA*. Greenwood's first award-winning instructional video featured her ex-husband, country singer Lee Greenwood. Melanie Greenwood has also served as a choreographer for Larry Gatlin and contemporary

Christian music singer Amy Grant, but one of her most famous creations is the Achy Breaky, a line dance timed to coincide with the release of Billy Ray Cyrus's recording of 'Achy Breaky Heart.'

The popularity of line dances (which allow any number of dancers to join in) such as the Achy Breaky and Boot Scootin' Boogie prompted Larry Boone to release a 1993 line-dance album, *Get In Line*, with the hope that dancers would use the LP's music as background to a Boone's line dance known as the Boone Walk.

It remains to be seen whether or not country line dancing is a fad. Thought to be a mutation of the conga line and the Harlem Hustle, forms of country line dancing include the Honky-Tonk Stomp, Neon Moon (as in the title of another Brooks and Dunn hit) and the Tush Push, variations being created almost as quickly as they can be named. Reminiscent of the pop music line dances of the Fifties, country line dancing is being dubbed the square dancing of the Nineties.

INSTRUMENTALS

Country's Most Neglected Music

COUNTRY MUSIC INSTRUMENTALS ARE AS OLD AS THE MUSIC ITSELF. COUNTRY SINGING AND DANCING HAS ALWAYS CALLED FOR MUSICAL ACCOMPANIMENT. NOT ONLY WAS THE GRAND OLE OPRY'S FIRST PERFORMER A FIDDLER, THE EARLIEST OPRY ROSTER CONSISTED MAINLY OF STRING BANDS. UNTIL 1938, WHEN ROY ACUFF JOINED THE OPRY, WHAT SINGERS THERE WERE ON THE SHOW WERE SUBORDINATES TO THE FEATURED BANDS OF THE DAY.

It wasn't long, though, before that trend was reversed. Record companies, as reflected by the contrast in sales and chart action between country's vocal versus its instrumental hits, have never promoted instrumentals with the same enthusiasm and tenacity they give to lyrical country songs.

Moreover, with the advent of country radio or, more specifically, commercial country radio, programming restrictions have evolved. The same forces which shape formats of shorter playlists (intensifying competition for air play) and dictate such practises as the de facto ban on airing ballads consecutively and songs longer than X number of minutes, tend to result in the greater difficulty of getting country instrumentals heard. Also, because they are tailor-made to be excerpted, country music instrumentals are customarily used as segues into news and commercial breaks. As a result, unless listeners buy

the CD, they may be unable to hear an instrumental all the way through.

There have, of course, been some notable exceptions. Back in 1946, Al Dexter had a Number 1 record with his instrumental, 'Guitar Polka.' A few years later Grand Ole Opry ragtime pianist Del Wood saw her 1951 signature song 'Down Yonder' go gold. By 1955, Chet Atkins was well on the way to becoming a household name. Atkins' instrumental recording of the Chordettes' 1954 pop hit 'Mr. Sandman' began a series of hit records over nearly three decades including 'Yakety Axe' (retitled 'Yakety Sax' when it became a pop hit for Boots Randolph in 1963), and 'Fiddlin' Around' (which featured sessions great Johnny Gimble on fiddle). Atkins still records, reuniting with an old duet partner, Jerry Reed, in 1992 to produce the LP *Sneakin' Around*.

In 1958, even Bill Monroe got into the act with 'Scotland,' just as earlier in the year Duane Eddy— "Mr. Twang"—topped both the pop and country charts with his signature song, 'Rebel-Rouser.' Two years later, pianist Floyd Cramer made both country and pop charts with his hit, 'Last Date.' Cramer's 'San Antonio Rose' was also a hit on both charts. By 1977, when Cramer released his version of the Cascades' 1963 pop hit 'Rhythm Of The Rain,' it was clear that his instrumentals knew no musical boundaries, a point Cramer drove home yet again in 1980 with 'Dallas,' the theme from the hit American TV series of the same name.

In 1970, a veteran record producer and trumpet player who had taken the stage name Danny Davis (real name George Nowlan) teamed with his group the Nashville Brass (formed in 1968) to record a series of instrumental hits lasting through the Eighties such as 'Columbus Stockade Blues' and 'How I Love Them Old Songs.'

In 1965, Buck Owens and the Buckaroos had their biggest instrumental hit, 'Buckaroo,' a Number 1 country record that crossed over to the pop charts. Owens' band went on to have several country

Singer, violinist and guitarist, Al Dexter had six other Number 1 hits besides his 'Piston Packin' Mama.'

instrumental releases of their own until 1970, including 'I'm Coming Back Home To Stay' and 'Nobody But You.'

Country's session players came into their own during the Seventies. Charlie McCoy, one of Nashville's greatest harmonica players, who was previously associated with the short-lived studio group Area Code 615 in 1969, had a big year in 1972 with instrumental versions of 'Today I Started Loving You Again,' 'I'm So Lonesome I Could Cry' and 'I

Really Don't Want To Know.' McCoy, who later became the musical director for *Hee Haw*, had a hit with another sessions group with an equally brief career in 1974 when Charlie McCoy and Barefoot Jerry scored with 'Boogie Woogie' (also called 'T. D.'s Boogie Woogie'). McCoy's recordings of 'Orange Blossom Special,' 'Shenandoah' and 'Release Me' continue to be among his most popular releases.

In 1973, session steel guitarist Lloyd Greene, who was featured on the Byrds' album *Sweethearts Of The Rodeo*, had country hits with instrumental covers of the pop hits 'I Can See Clearly Now' and 'Here Comes The Sun.'

Roy Clark had an instrumental hit in 1983 with 'Riders In The Sky,' but the bulk of Clark's hits have not been instrumentals, demonstrating the subordinate status of instrumentals in country music.

Still, instrumentals are far from dead, as evidenced by session veteran and award-winning soloist Mark O'Connor, who has repopularized fiddle music.

ROY ACUFF

See separate entry in the Legends section.

ALABAMA

In 1979 a mixture of curiosity and excitement began to circulate about a quartet of long-haired country boys who had a hit record with their first release on the second of two small labels with which they had signed. The song was 'I Wanna Come Over' and the group was Alabama. Formed in 1969 as Wild Country, the Fort Payne, Alabama-based group's national popularity evolved from the interest it sparked working clubs in and around Myrtle Beach, South Carolina beginning in 1973.

The three original members are cousins from Fort Payne: lead vocalist Randy Owen (born on December 13, 1949), Jeffrey Cook, lead guitar and fiddle (born on August 27, 1949) and Teddy Gentry (born on January 22, 1952). Since its formation, the group has had only one personnel change. In 1976 Wild Fire's drummer, John Vartanian, was replaced by the group's only Yankee, Mark Herndon (born May 11, 1955 in Springfield, Massachusetts). The following year Wild Fire changed its name to

Alabama—Randy, Jeff, Mark and Teddy: the quartet that put Fort Payne on the map.

Alabama, obtaining its first recording contract. As Alabama, the group immediately took a personal interest in their work, producing and promoting their first records. So it wasn't surprising that by 1980, 'My Home's In Alabama', Alabama's second release for the independent MDJ record label, was selling so well that RCA Records made contractual arrangements to take over the distribution of 'My Home's In Alabama,' while signing the newcomers to its label for future record production.

That arrangement worked well, for Alabama has had a string of Number 1 country records that have also charted pop. Some of these are 'Feels So Right,' 'Take Me Down' and 'The Closer You Get.'

Named in 1989 as the Academy of Country Music's Artists of the Decade, Alabama is also the ACM's five-time Entertainer(s) of the Year, and, in 1993, Alabama became an 11-time winner of the American Music Awards' Best Country Duo or Group honors (the longest run of consecutive wins of any act in any category in the 20-year history of the AMA).

Alabama has also released nearly 40 hit singles (including 'Face To Face,' featuring K. T. Oslin) from its gold and multi-platinum selling LPs, racking up a staggering total of 50 million albums sold worldwide.

Alabama is generous with its wealth, donating to local charities in and around Fort Payne by means of funds raised at the June Jam, so named to denote the date it occurs and the aspect of informality and sharing between all the big-name country acts who appear at the concert which draws fans from all over America and beyond.

BILL ANDERSON

Bill Anderson's soft, slightly nasal voice is as unique as his contributions to country music have been. A good sport, Bill jokes about the fan who told him, in all sincerity, that she hoped the perfectly healthy entertainer would soon "get rid of your cold."

James William Anderson III was born on November 1, 1937 in Columbia, South Carolina. By the time Bill began the fourth grade his middle-class family moved first to Griffin, Georgia and then on to Decatur where, at the age of 15, Anderson and some Avondale high school buddies formed a band called the Avondale Playboys. The group had its own Saturday morning radio show on nearby Atlanta's WBGE Radio and, while still in high school, Bill was also sports editor for a Decatur weekly newspaper.

While pursuing a journalism degree from the University of Georgia, Anderson spent summer breaks as a country music disc jockey. One of the places Bill worked was Commerce, Georgia's WJJC radio. It was on the back of a station envelope that 19-year-old Bill Anderson wrote 'City Lights,' the song that became a Number 1 record for Ray Price in 1958 and launched Anderson on a successful career of his own. Bill signed with Decca (now MCA) Records and recorded his first hit, 'That's What It's Like to Be Lonesome' that same year.

With six hits to his credit, Bill joined the Grand Ole Opry in 1961. The following year, Anderson had a

Number 1 hit with 'Mama Sang A Song,' a tune that incorporated a spoken line. Bill's signature song, 'Still,' released in 1963, combined his vocal with a recitation, leading Don Bowman to dub the softspoken Anderson "Whisperin' Bill."

With scores of chart singles to his credit (both as a solo artist and as the duet partner of Jan Howard, Mary Lou Turner, David Allan Coe and Roy Acuff), Anderson's pen has won him over 50 BMI songwriting awards, making him one of the most honored songwriters in country music history.

The first country artist to host a game show (ABC TV's *The Better Sex*), Bill also discovered Opry star Connie Smith, whose signature song is the Anderson composition 'Once A Day.'

Anderson is an alternating host of *Opry Backstage*, the TNN interview show preceding the weekly televised portion of the Grand Ole Opry.

Bill has written his autobiography, *Whisperin' Bill*, has a second untitled book of "road stories" set for publication, and is working on his first novel.

EDDY ARNOLD

See separate entry in the Legends section.

Chet Atkins—"Mr Guitar"—winner of umpteen instrumentalist of the year honors.

CHET ATKINS

Voted into the Country Music Hall of Fame in 1973, Chet Atkins was, at 49, its youngest inductee.

Born in Luttrell, Tennessee on June 20, 1924, Chester Burton Atkins began a career as a musician that would earn him international fame and the title of "Mr Guitar" in 1942, performing on Knoxville, Tennessee radio station WNOX.

After touring with WNOX radio stars Bill Carlisle and Archie Campbell (Atkins played fiddle and guitar), Chet spent the next 2 years at WLW in Cincinnati before moving on to Red Foley's Chicago-based radio program.

In 1946, Atkins became a recording artist moving from the Bullet label to RCA Victor (in Chicago) in 1947, but it wasn't until 1950 that Chet actually moved to Nashville. During the Fifties, Atkins became a regular on the Grand Ole Opry, entertaining there when he was not recording or working as a musician on some of Nashville's earliest recording sessions (including Hank Williams'), or producing the acts he signed to RCA (Waylon Jennings, Jim Reeves, Don Gibson and Willie Nelson among others) which would later bring him the credit for being one of the originators of the Nashville Sound.

As an artist, Atkins has recorded over 75 albums. His duet partners have included Jerry Reed, Hank Snow, Merle Travis, Les Paul, Doc Watson and Mark Knopfler.

Atkins took on the title of RCA A & R manager from 1960 to 1968, and from 1968 until 1981 was a vice-president for the label. In 1982, Atkins signed a recording contract with CBS Records. Chet's autobiography, *Chet Atkins, Country Gentleman* was published in 1974.

For all Chet's accolades and corporate titles (in 1991 the section of South Street that runs through Nashville's Music Row was renamed "Chet Atkins Place"), the Grammy award-winning instrumentalist, presented with the National Association of Recording Arts and Sciences "Lifetime Achievement" award in 1993, relishes most the title he has given himself: CGP. It stands for "Certified Guitar Player."

BOBBY BARE

Whoever coined the term "laid back" must have had Bobby Bare in mind. Bare, whose favorite hobby is fishing, is rarely other than casually dressed. And, queried about his Opry membership status, Bobby presumes he is still a member, since he's never formally left (Bare has not performed on the Opry since it moved from the Ryman Auditorium to its present Opryland location in 1974).

Robert Joseph Bare was born on April 7, 1935 in Ironton, Ohio. Bare began singing professionally and working with bands at the age of 17, before moving on to California and Hawaii in 1953.

By 1956 Bobby was recording for Capitol Records but, having no success there, he had few qualms when, in 1958, he received his draft notice, shortly after having recorded a demo tape of a song spoofing Elvis Presley's career. That demo, a rocker called 'The All American Boy,' was recorded with Bobby's buddy, Bill Parsons, at the same session. Just as Bare had left for the Army, Cincinnati's Fraternity Records purchased all of the session tapes, each recording listing Bill Parsons as the artist! Only when Bobby heard himself singing 'The All American Boy' on the radio did the serviceman realize a mistake had been made. (To this day the record label still carries Parsons' name rather than Bare's.)

In 1962, Bare signed with RCA Records, recording some 70 charting records for RCA and other labels. 'Marie Laveau' is his biggest hit as a solo artist. He has had several duet partners including his wife Jeannie and their children (the Bares' late daughter Cari, and sons Shannon and Bobby, Jr), Skeeter Davis, Rosanne Cash, Lacy J. Dalton, Norma Jean and Liz Anderson. He has won several awards including a Grammy, two silver records from Norway and a gold disc from South Africa.

Tourists can often find Bobby at The Bare Trap, a Nashville area souvenir shop specializing in stuffed teddy bears named after celebrities. Bare is a spokesperson for Red Man Tobacco.

Clint Black, usually one of country music's "hatted hunks," now sometimes goes hatless.

CLINT BLACK

The youngest of four brothers, Clint Black was born in Houston, Texas, in February 4, 1962. Dropping out from high school, he started singing in clubs, such gigs being his only source of income for 8 years. When his first single, 'A Better Man,' was released in 1989, it marked the first time in 15 years that a male country artist had achieved the feat of a Number 1 hit with his first release.

Clint scored another first when 'A Better Man' turned out to be the first of no fewer than five Number 1 singles (the others were 'Killin' Time,' 'Nobody's Home,' 'Walking Away' and 'Nothing's News') from one album, the double platinum-selling *Killin' Time*. Black's second album, *Put Yourself In My Shoes*, was also certified double platinum.

Clint released a third album, *The Hard Way* (featuring 'We Tell Ourselves' and 'When My Ship Comes In') in 1992. He bears a strong resemblance, but is no relation, to Roy Rogers, and has recorded the hit 'Hold On Partner' with Rogers.

Clint, the Country Music Association's 1989 Horizon Award-winner and 1990 Male Vocalist of the Year recipient, co-writes many of his songs with his collaborator and lead guitarist, Hayden Nicholas.

GARTH BROOKS

See separate entry in the Legends section.

JIM ED BROWN

Smooth-voiced Jim Ed Brown can boast three careers: one with his sisters, his solo career, and another as the duet partner of Helen Cornelius.

Born on April Fool's Day, 1934 in Sparkman, Arkansas, Brown performed during the Forties on Pine Bluff, Arkansas's KCLA Radio. Jim Ed's older sister Maxine also performed on KCLA, but the siblings didn't come together as a duo until 1953 when they won an amateur contest in Little Rock, Arkansas. Subsequently Jim Ed and Maxine appeared on the *Louisiana Hayride* and Red Foley's *Ozark Jubilee*. and in 1954 they scored a Top 10 country hit with a record titled 'Looking Back to See.' The following year Jim Ed did the same thing with 'Here Today and Gone Tomorrow', but this time in partnership with younger sister Bonnie. In 1955 Bonnie joined

Jim Ed and Maxine to form a trio called the Browns. They signed with RCA and had their first hits with 'I Take The Chance', 'The Three Bells', 'Scarlet Ribbons' and 'The Old Lamplighter.'

By the time the Browns disbanded in 1967, Jim Ed was already a Grand Ole Opry member and had been having hits as a solo act since 1965. With hits such as 'Pop A Top,' 'Morning' and 'Southern Loving,' Brown's solo career has continued, interrupted between 1976 and 1981 by a duet partnership with Helen Cornelius.

During that partnership, Brown and Cornelius had 13 chart singles, including their biggest hits, 'I Don't Want To Have To Marry You,' 'Saying Hello, Saying I Love You, Saying Goodbye,' and 'Lying In Love With You.'

Glen Campbell may have a baby face but he's been around a long time on the country scene.

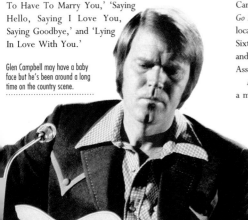

ARCHIE CAMPBELL

Archie Campbell is best remembered as one of the television series *Hee Haw*'s ensemble cast of comedians (he was also the show's chief writer). But Archie was so much more. Not only a great storyteller, Campbell was a master of spoonerisms: a sort of fractured English that made Archie's tales of "Rindercella", "Beeping Sleauty" and "The Pee Little Thrigs" much funnier than the fairy tales that inspired them.

Born in Bulls Gap, Tennessee, on November 7, 1914, Campbell began his career on Knoxville's *Mid-day Merry Go Round* during the Thirties and Forties and had his own local TV show in Knoxville during the Fifties. During the Sixties he recorded for RCA Records, both as a solo act and with Lorene Mann, winning the Country Music Association's "Comedian of the Year" award in 1969.

Archie joined the Grand Ole Opry in 1958 and was a member until his death on August 29, 1987.

GLEN CAMPBELL

Glen Travis Campbell was born in Billstown, Arkansas on April 22, 1936. When he was 4 his father bought him a $5 Sears Roebuck guitar. Within 2 years Campbell had mastered the instrument. At 14, the pride of his home town, Campbell left home for Albuquerque, New Mexico, where he played in his uncle Dick Bills' three-piece band, later forming his own band before moving to California in 1960 and establishing himself there as a studio musician (Campbell was on the Champs' 'Tequila' session in 1960, and, following studio work with the Beach Boys in 1965, occasionally toured with them, substituting for Brian Wilson).

Glen released a single on a regional label in 1961 and was subsequently signed by Capitol Records which, in 1962, released a Top 20 country record called 'Kentucky Means Paradise' by the Green River Boys, featuring Glen. In 1966 his cover of Jack Scott's 1960 pop hit 'Burning Bridges' reached Number 18 on *Billboard*'s country charts, but it was the following year that Glen first released 'Gentle On My Mind' (Campbell re-released the John Hartford composition in 1968). 'Gentle On My Mind' not only became Glen's signature song, it remains one of the most played in country music's history.

With crossover hits such as 'By The Time I Get To Phoenix,' 'Wichita Lineman' and 'Galveston,' Campbell entertained audiences on his own CBS TV series, *The Glen Campbell Goodtime Hour* from 1968 through 1972. He went on briefly to host a syndicated TV series and established a movie career with film credits including *True Grit*, *Norwood* and *Strange Homecoming*.

Known as the "Rhinestone Cowboy" (the title of Campbell's 1975 gold record), Glen, the Country Music Association's 1968 Entertainer of the Year, is also a five-time Grammy award winner.

MARY-CHAPIN CARPENTER

When she was born in Princeton, New Jersey on February 21, 1958, the singer's given name was Mary Chapin Carpenter (a combination of her parents' names). Carpenter's record label added the hyphen so that Mary-Chapin would be called by her proper name (an exercise in futility, for she is still erroneously called Mary, though her nickname is Chapin).

A graduate of Brown University, Mary-Chapin signed with Columbia Records in 1986. Her hits have included 'Quittin' Time' and 'Passionate Kisses.' Another favorite is an esoteric ditty called 'Opening Act' which is a sardonic view of what it's like being overshadowed by a

Mary-Chapin Carpenter—Ivy League country at its best.

headliner. Chapin's duet performance with Joe Diffie ('Not Too Much To Ask') was nominated for a Grammy Award in 1992.

Carpenter won the Grammy category of Best Country Vocal Performance, Female in 1991 for her Cajun-flavored single, 'Down At The Twist And Shout,' and in 1992 Best Country Vocal Performance, Female for 'I Feel Lucky.'

In 1993, Chapin's album *Come On Come On* received platinum certification.

THE CARTER FAMILY

The Carter Family—Maybelle, Sara and A. P. Carter were the "First Family of Country Music."

A.P., Sara and Maybelle are sometimes called the Original Carter Family to distinguish them from their children and grandchildren. Known as the "First Family of Country Music," they were among the first musicians to play and record country music. The Carters made country music history on June 10, 1931 when they recorded with Jimmie Rodgers.

Virginians Alvin Pleasant Carter (1891–1960) from Maces Springs, his wife Sara (1899–1979) from Copper Creek, and Sara's cousin, Maybelle (1909–78) from Nicklesville, recorded some 300 songs during the period between 1928 and 1941.

A.P. played the fiddle and wrote or adapted many of the trio's songs, including 'Wildwood Flower.' Sara sang lead and played guitar, banjo and autoharp. Maybelle sang alto and played several instruments (including guitar with a "drop-thumb" technique), but Mother Maybelle—as she came to be known in later years—is best remembered for popularizing the autoharp.

For 6 months in 1942, when the Original Carters were entertaining on Charlotte, North Carolina station WBT, the family formally expanded to include A.P. and Sara's children, Gladys, Janette and Joe, as well as Maybelle's children, Helen, June and Anita. The children had made their singing débuts on XERA, a time during which A.P. and Sara divorced and Sara remarried, leading to the professional break-up of the Original Carter Family.

Each of the Original Carters came out of retirement at various times, performing not with each other, but with their children. Some of the children of these children have, in turn, performed under the Carter name, so creating a truly amazing country music dynasty.

JOHNNY CASH

See separate entry in the Legends section.

ROSANNE CASH

Rosanne Cash, the eldest of Johnny Cash and his first wife Vivian's four daughters, was born in Memphis, Tennessee, on May 24, 1955. Raised in California by her mother, Rosanne moved to Nashville following her high school graduation. Cash enjoyed the proximity to her father, occasionally joining him on tour. During the Seventies when the elder Cash was already a TV star, Rosanne acted as his wardrobe mistress and filled in at Johnny's House of Cash offices.

Rosanne's first recording, a duet with Bobby Bare called 'No Memories Hangin' Round,' was released in 1979. A 1985 Grammy winner (Best Country Vocal Performance, Female for 'I Don't Know Why You Don't Want Me') Cash has had 11 Number 1 solo hits, including 'Seven Year Ache' and 'The Way We Make A Broken Heart', and in 1988 a Number 1 duet with her then-husband Rodney Crowell, 'It's Such A Small World'.

TOMMY CASH

Tommy Cash was born April 5, 1940 in Dyess, Arkansas.

While in the Army, stationed in Frankfurt, Germany, Cash worked as a country music disc jockey on the American Armed Forces Network. Returning to the States, he worked for Memphis radio station KWAM before moving to Nashville in 1964 to manage his brother Johnny's publishing company.

Tommy began recording in 1968 and had the biggest hit of his career, 'Six White Horses' (a tribute to John Kennedy, Martin Luther King, Jr and Robert Kennedy), the following year.

Over the next decade Cash had several big records including 'Rise and Shine,' 'That Certain One' and 'I'm Gonna Write A Song.'

During the Seventies Tommy was one of the Nashville Pickers, a baseball team composed of country music stars like Roy Clark, Jerry Reed, Johnny Duncan, Bob Luman, Charley Pride, Bill Anderson and Eddy Raven who visited major league parks to compete against the home team's local media personalities before the big game.

In the Nineties, Cash is one of several performers fans can expect to see when they visit country music's performance Mecca, Branson, Missouri.

ROY CLARK

The host of the erstwhile *Hee Haw* since the program's début in 1969, Roy Linwood Clark was born in Meherrin, Virginia on April 15, 1933.

After winning the National Country Music Banjo Competition in 1947 and 1948, Clark became a regular on the TV series starring his mentor Jimmy Dean, and George Hamilton IV. Roy also appeared as "Cousin Roy" and his mother as "Big Mama Halsey" (Clark's manager was Jim Halsey) in the popular TV series *The Beverly Hillbillies*.

The Country Music Association's 1967 Entertainer of the Year, Roy plays more than half a dozen instruments. Hits such as 'Tips of My Fingers' and 'Yesterday When I Was Young' led Roy to the Soviet Union in 1976, where he played sold-out concerts in Moscow, Leningrad and Riga.

A Grand Ole Opry member since 1987, Roy lends his name to an annual charity golf tournament that has raised over $1 million for Tulsa, Oklahoma's Children's Medical Care Center.

PATSY CLINE

See separate entry in the Legends section.

EARL THOMAS CONLEY

Earl Thomas Conley was born on October 17, 1941 in Portsmouth, Ohio.

Conley was the first recording artist in any form of music to have four Number 1 singles released from the same album (1983's *Don't Make It Easy For Me*).

ETC, as he is known, wrote 'Smokey Mountain Memories,' Mel Street's 1975 hit, and 'This Time I've Hurt Her More Than She Needs Me,' Conway Twitty's Number 1 hit of the same year which became a hit again for Neal McCoy in 1992.

Conley's Number 1 hits as a solo artist include 'Fire And Smoke,' 'Your Love's On The Line,' and 'Holding Her And Loving You.' As a duet artist, Conley has also had hit records with Gus Hardin, Anita Pointer, Emmylou Harris and Keith Whitley.

Despite many record-setting accomplishments, Earl Thomas Conley remains one of country's most underrated talents.

BILLY RAY CYRUS

Billy Ray Cyrus, a native of Flatwoods, Kentucky, was born on August 25, 1961.

At the age of 20, Cyrus abandoned his hope of a career as a professional baseball player and bought a guitar. Soon Billy Ray and his band, Sly Dog, were the house band at Ironton, Ohio's Sand Bar.

In 1984, fire destroyed the band's equipment, which Cyrus took as a sign to move on: first to Los Angeles and then to Huntington, West Virginia where he spent 5 years as the nightly headliner at the Ragtime Lounge. Driving to Nashville on his days off, Cyrus connected with

Billy Ray Cyrus brings high energy rockin' (and a pony tail) to country music.

Grand Ole Opry star Del Reeves's daughter, Kari. Before long, Del Reeves cut one of Billy Ray's songs and secured a manager for him who, in turn, got Cyrus a record deal.

Billy Ray's first single, 'Achy Breaky Heart,' a Number 1 pop and country hit, made the charts before it was ever released and *Some Gave All*, the album on which it appears, was the first album ever to début on *Billboard*'s country album chart at Number 1 where it stayed for 18 consecutive weeks. Selling over 10 million copies, it remained at Number 1 on *Billboard*'s Top 200 chart longer than any other début album by an artist in any genre!

Some Gave All has received sales awards in the UK, Canada and New Zealand and was a hit in Australia, Belgium, Denmark, Japan and South Africa. Cyrus's other hits include 'Could've Been Me' and 'Where'm I Gonna Live,' from his first album.

CHARLIE DANIELS

Born in Wilmington, North Carolina, on October 28, 1936, Charlie Daniels was a self-taught fiddler and guitarist at the age of 15.

A Nashville session player during the late Sixties, the leader of the Charlie Daniels Band made a name for himself playing southern rock classics such as 'The South's Gonna Do

It Again' and a fiddle tune, 'The Devil Went Down To Georgia,' a gold record for Daniels in 1979.

A charity fund-raiser known as the Charlie Daniels Volunteer Jam, showcasing country, rock, blues and classical music, has been a largely annual event since 1974 and attracts fans from all over the world.

SKEETER DAVIS

Mary Frances Penick was given the nickname "Skeeter" (as in mosquito) by her grandfather. Davis was the last name of Skeeter's best friend and singing partner Betty Jack. Betty Jack and Skeeter were professionally known as the Davis Sisters and had a gold record with 'I Forgot More Than You'll Ever Know.'

Born in Dry Ridge, Kentucky on December 30, 1931, Skeeter began her solo career following Betty Jack's fatal car accident in 1953 after first unsuccessfully trying to keep the Davis Sisters going with Betty Jack's sister, Georgia.

Skeeter toured with Eddy Arnold and Elvis Presley and has had over 40 records on both the country and pop charts, including 'My Last Date (With You)' and 'The

Charlie Daniels—an outspoken southern rocker and founder of the world-famous Volunteer Jam.

End Of The World.' Davis has recorded duets with Bobby Bare, Don Bowman and George Hamilton IV.

Her autobiography, *Bus Fare To Kentucky* (titled after one of her hits), was published in 1993.

JIMMY DEAN

Jimmy Dean, known as the "Sausage King" because a well known American sausage-making company bears the same name, was born on August 10, 1928 in Plainview, Texas.

After recording his first hit, 'Bumming Around,' in 1953, Dean was the star of his own prime-time summer show in 1957 as well as a half-hour daytime CBS TV series that ran from April through December 1957 and September 1958 through June 1959 (both shows came out of Washington, DC). *The Jimmy Dean Show* was an ABC TV variety hour from 1963 through 1966, and Dean had a syndicated TV show from 1973 through 1975.

Dean's signature song, 'Big Bad John,' a Number 1 pop and country hit in 1961, was a gold record, as was 'IOU,' a recitation Dean recorded in 1976. (The latter was reissued, charting again in 1977 and 1983.)

Jimmy Dean will always be remembered for his contributions to country.

LITTLE JIMMY DICKENS

The youngest of 13 children, 4-ft. 11-in. James Cecil Dickens was born on December 19, 1920 in Bolt, West Virginia.

In 1942, Dickens got his start as "Jimmy the Kid" with Johnny Bailes and his Happy Valley Boys. In 1948 he joined the Grand Ole Opry. Nicknamed "Tater" following the 1949 release of his hit 'Take An Old Cold Tater (And Wait),' Dickens had hits including 'A-Sleeping At

The Foot Of The Bed' and his biggest, a novelty number called 'May The Bird of Paradise Fly Up Your Nose.' Jimmy Dickens was elected to the Country Music Hall of Fame in 1982.

Dickens oversees "The Tater Patch," a concession booth serving potato soup, baked potatoes and French fries, as he joins several Grand Ole Opry stars welcoming visitors to Nashville's Opryland theme park, signing autographs, and posing for photos with fans.

DAVE DUDLEY

Born David Pedruska in Spencer, Wisconsin on May 3, 1928, Dudley played semi-pro baseball until he injured his arm.

After working as a singer and a disc jockey at Wausau, Wisconsin's WTWT Radio in 1950, Dudley formed a trio and worked throughout the midwestern United States, becoming a solo artist by 1961.

Known for his truck drivin' songs, Dudley recorded his signature song, 'Six Days On The Road,' in 1963. In appreciation of his work, Nashville's truckers' union presented Dave with a gold union card.

Dave's other hits have included 'Mad,' 'What We're Fighting For' and 'The Pool Shark,' all written by Tom T. Hall with whom Dudley recorded the 1970 hit 'Day Drinkin'.'

FREDDY FENDER

Born Baldemar Huerta on June 4, 1937 in San Benito, Texas, Freddy Fender's first (Spanish) releases in 1956 were recorded under his real name.

Fender (taking his name from the famous guitar) was a New Orleans session musician during the Sixties. He was one of the top country acts of 1975 with two gold singles, 'Before The Next Teardrop Falls' (a bilingual recording alternating English and Spanish verses like Johnny Rodriguez does in 'Love Me With All Of Your Heart') and 'Wasted Days And Wasted Nights' on ABC/Dot. Fender first recorded the latter for a small label in 1959.

Today, the Tex-Mex star is a member of the Texas Tornados, whose Tejano music is a hybrid of the traditional Mexican mariachi music and country music.

TENNESSEE ERNIE FORD

"Bless your little pea-pickin' hearts," was Ernest Jennings Ford's famous homespun expression of gratitude.

Ford, who was born in Bristol, Tennessee on February 13, 1919, worked for radio stations in Bristol, Atlanta, Georgia, Knoxville, Tennessee, San Bernardino and Pasadena, California before singing with Cliffie Stone's quartet on the Hometown Jamboree.

Ford became a recording artist in 1948

Tennessee Ernie Ford—country gospel's favourite pea-picker.

having hits like 'Mule Train,' 'The Shotgun Boogie' and his 1955 signature song, 'Sixteen Tons.'

Tennessee Ernie hosted his NBC TV musical variety show from 1956 to 1961 and later turned to recording gospel music.

Ford was inducted into the Country Music Hall of Fame in 1990 and died on October 17, 1991.

LEFTY FRIZZELL

Nicknamed Lefty during his amateur boxing career, William Orville Frizzell was born March 31, 1928 in Corsicana, Texas.

Frizzell dominated the charts during 1950 and 1951 with Number 1 hits such as 'If You've Got The Money I've Got The Time,' 'I Love You A Thousand Ways' and 'Always Late (With Your Kisses).'

After a quarter-century career of recording songs in a honky-tonk style that influenced singers such as Merle Haggard, George Jones and Randy Travis, Frizzell suffered a stroke and died in Nashville on July 19, 1975.

Lefty was posthumously elected to the Country Music Hall of Fame in 1982 and a bronze statue of him was erected in Corsicana in 1992.

Crystal Gayle: ankle-length locks have not distracted fans from the artistry of Loretta Lynn's little sister.

CRYSTAL GAYLE

Born in Paintsville, Kentucky on January 9, 1951 and raised in Wabash, Indiana, Brenda Gail Webb was given the stage name Crystal Gayle by her sister, Loretta Lynn.

At the age of 16, Brenda began singing with Loretta's road show. In 1970, signing with Decca Records, Brenda took her stage name—Crystal comes from the Krystal hamburger chain—so as to avoid confusion with labelmate, Brenda Lee.

The first country artist to tour China (1979), Crystal's string of hit records includes 'I'll Get Over You,' her gold single, 'Don't It Make My Brown Eyes Blue' and a remake of Johnnie Ray's 'Cry.'

Her Number 1 duets include 'You and I' (with Eddie Rabbitt) and 'Making Up For Lost Time (The Dallas Lovers' Song)' (with Gary Morris).

DON GIBSON

Donald Eugene Gibson was born on April 3, 1928 in Shelby, North Carolina.

Gibson began his career working local clubs and performing on radio while still in high school, moving to Knoxville, Tennessee in 1953 to appear on WNOX Radio's *Tennessee Barn Dance* and *Midday Merry-Go-Round*. One of country music's most prolific songwriters,

Gibson wrote and recorded hits such as 'Sweet Dreams,' 'Oh Lonesome Me,' and 'I Can't Stop Loving You,' before joining the Grand Ole Opry in 1958. From 1956 through 1970, Gibson had over 80 chart singles, including duets with Dottie West and Sue Thompson. He is a member of the Songwriters Hall of Fame.

VINCE GILL

Vincent Grant Gill was born on April 12, 1957 in Norman, Oklahoma.

Vince became a guitarist at the age of 10 and at 15 he was the vocalist/lead guitarist for his own band. A scratch golfer, Gill once wanted to play pro golf, but instead joined Sam Bush's group, Bluegrass Alliance, in 1975. He then played in Boone Creek (with Ricky Skaggs) and yet another bluegrass group, Sundance (with Byron Berline) before becoming the lead singer of the rock group Pure Prairie League. (Mark Knopfler later

Vince Gill, one of country's busiest session players, has now taken center stage.

tried unsuccessfully to recruit Vince for his group, Dire Straits.) Gill joined Rodney Crowell's band, the Cherry Bombs, in 1982 and the tenor harmony singer did session work in Nashville as he launched his solo career on RCA Records in 1984.

Gill's 'I Still Believe In You' was judged the best country song of 1992 by both the National Academy of Recording Arts and Sciences and the Music City News Country Songwriters Awards. The Grammy and CMA Award-winning entertainer was also named BMI's Country Songwriter of the Year in 1992 for placing 'Look At Us,' 'Pocket Full of Gold,' 'Liza Jane' and 'Here We Are' on the performing rights organization's most performed list.

A Grand Ole Opry member since 1991, Vince is known for his civic involvement. He participated in, and was the honorary chairman of, DreamMakers' 1993 Celebrity Waiters' Luncheon (raising money to grant the wishes of terminally-ill children). Vince was also the 1993 national spokesperson for the EAR Foundation (an organization dedicated to helping the hearing-impaired).

JACK GREENE

Country music's hottest act in 1967 was Jack Greene. That year the leader of his own group, the Jolly Giants, joined the Grand Ole Opry, won the CMA's Male Vocalist of the Year, Single of the Year and Album of the Year awards on the strength of his first Number 1 record and one of two signature songs, 'There Goes My Everything.'

Jack Henry Greene was born in Maryville, Tennessee on January 7, 1930. Greene worked with Atlanta's Cherokee Trio during the Forties and the Rhythm Ranch Boys and the Peachtree Cowboys during the Fifties, prior to joining Ernest Tubb's Texas Troubadours, fronting the band and playing drums, in 1962.

By 1965, Greene had signed with Decca Records and began to have many hits including 'All The Time,' 'You Are My Treasure' and another signature song, 'Statue of A Fool.'

For 11 years Jack toured and sang with fellow Opry star Jeannie Seely. Their hit duets include 'Wish I Didn't Have To Miss You,' 'Much Oblige' and 'What In The World Has Gone Wrong With Our Love.'

NANCI GRIFFITH

Nanci Griffith was born in Austin, Texas on July 6, 1954.

At 14, Griffith began singing in clubs. Having learned to play guitar, she continued to moonlight at bars while earning a degree in education from the University of Texas which she put to good use by teaching kindergarten and first grade in Austin.

By the late Seventies Griffith decided to pursue music exclusively, recording her first album *There's A Light*

Europe, rather than America, has recognized Nanci Griffith as a country singer.

Beyond These Woods (1978). Nanci's recording of Julie Gold's 'From A Distance' became a Number 1 hit in Ireland years before Bette Midler's version was an American hit.

As a songwriter, Griffith's credits include Kathy Mattea's 'Love At The Five And Dime' and Suzy Boggus's 'Outbound Plane.'

Dubbed "Queen of Folkabilly" by *Rolling Stone* magazine, Grammy nominee Griffith has won several European awards, including the IRMA and the Edison Award, and has appeared at the London Palladium.

Nanci is a platinum-selling artist in England and Ireland. She calls Ireland her second home, recording, writing or performing there several months each year.

MERLE HAGGARD

Merle Ronald Haggard was born in an abandoned railroad car on April 6, 1937 near Bakersfield, California.

Two years after being named the Country Music Association's 1970 Entertainer of the Year, he was granted a full pardon by California Governor Ronald Reagan for an attempted burglary conviction that had resulted in a spell in San Quentin from 1957 through 1960.

When Johnny Cash first performed at San Quentin, Haggard was in the front row. During the Sixties, Merle formed a band called the Strangers (named for his 1965 hit '(My Friends Are Gonna Be) Strangers'), and, along with Buck Owens, put Bakersfield on the map as a country music center.

Among Haggard's nearly 40 Number 1 records are 'The Fugitive,' 'Branded Man,'

Merle Haggard, the Country Music Association's most nominated artist of all time.

51

'Mama Tried,' and Merle's signature song, 'Okie From Muskogee.'

The Hag's duet partners have included Clint Eastwood, Janie Frickie, George Jones, Willie Nelson, Bonnie Owens (both his and Buck Owens's ex-wife), Johnny Paycheck and Leona Williams (another of his ex-wives).

Merle's autobiography, *Sing Me Back Home: My Life* was published in 1981.

With 42 nominations, Haggard holds the record as the CMA's most-nominated country artist of all time.

TOM T. HALL

Dubbed "the Storyteller" by Tex Ritter to characterize his style of story-songwriting and performing, Thomas Hall (his full name) was born on May 25, 1936 in Tick Ridge, Kentucky.

Many of Tom's hits are based on real-life experiences including 'Ballad Of Forty Dollars' (culled from his army service in Germany), 'The Year That Clayton Delaney Died' (Tom's reminiscence about losing his childhood hero) and his signature song 'I Love' (a lyrical listing of what Tom holds most dear).

Jimmy Newman was one of the first to believe in Hall's work and to record his songs which, over the years, have also been recorded by George Kent, Johnny Wright, Bobby Bare, Dave Dudley, Johnny Cash, George Jones, Burl Ives, Tommy Cash and many others.

A 1972 Grammy winner (for Best Album Notes—*Tom T. Hall's Greatest Hits*) and five-time CMA Award nominee (1973), Hall is best known as the writer of Jeannie C. Riley's 1968 Number 1 pop and country hit, 'Harper Valley P.T.A.'

Tom's duet partners have included Dave Dudley, Patti Page and Earl Scruggs.

Now retired from the road with 46 BMI songwriter awards in his pocket, Hall has turned to writing novels. He has also published his memoirs (*The Storyteller's Nashville*), a children's book, a handbook for songwriters, and a book of short stories.

GEORGE HAMILTON IV

An international favorite, singer George Hamilton IV has scored several firsts.

He was the first American country singer to record an album in Eastern Europe and to tour Russia and Czechoslovakia (1974). He was the first to have his own BBC TV series in the UK (George has now hosted a total of nine such series, including three in Belfast, Northern Ireland). And he was also present at the first major country music festivals outside the US: Wembley, UK (1969), Sweden (1976), Finland (1977), Norway and Holland (1978), Germany (1979), Switzerland and France (1980) and Austria (1984).

George Hege Hamilton IV was born on July 19, 1937 in Winston-Salem, North Carolina. He became a teen idol

Mild-mannered George Hamilton IV is not as fully appreciated in the US as he is in other parts of the world.

with the release of his first hit, 'A Rose And A Baby Ruth,' in 1956 and he toured with Buddy Holly, the Everly Brothers and Gene Vincent.

Moving to Nashville in 1959, George joined the Grand Ole Opry for the first time in 1960. He joined again in 1976 after 5 years' television work in North Carolina, Canada and Great Britain. Nicknamed "the Number" for the Roman numeral IV he wears on his vest pocket, Hamilton named his band "the Numbers."

Tourists have George and songwriter John D. Loudermilk (co-writer of Hamilton's signature song, 'Abilene') to thank for helping to originate the "homes of the stars" bus tours available in Nashville today.

EMMYLOU HARRIS

Born in Birmingham, Alabama on April 2, 1947, Emmylou Harris began her career in the Washington, DC area as a folksinger during the Sixties. In 1969 she began recording and toured with Gram Parsons and the Flying Burrito Brothers until 1973. Two years later Harris formed her own Hot band which featured Rodney Crowell and Ricky Skaggs (but never Vince Gill, according to Harris).

Emmylou began having her first hits in 1975 when 'If I Could Only Win Your Love' reached Number 4 in *Billboard*. Many more hits followed, including 'Two More Bottles of Wine' and 'Beneath Still Waters.'

In 1987 Emmylou, Dolly Parton and Linda Ronstadt, billing themselves as Trio, covered the Teddy Bears' 1958 hit 'To Know Him Is To Love Him.' Emmylou's duet partners have included Earl Thomas Conley, John Denver, Charlie Louvin, Roy Orbison, Buck Owens and Don Williams.

A Grand Ole Opry member since 1991, Harris and her acoustic band, the Nash Ramblers, released a Grammy Award-winning album recorded on the Ryman stage that same year.

Harris has served as both the president and as a trustee of the Country Music Foundation.

Emmylou Harris: Emmy preserves the folk sounds of country music.

ALAN JACKSON

One of country music's "hatted hunks," lanky blond Alan Eugene Jackson was born October 17, 1958 in Newnam, Georgia. Arriving in Nashville at the age of 25, he landed his first day job in the Nashville Network mail room. His wife, Denise, then an airline attendant, met a representative of Glen Campbell's music publishing company who gave Denise his card. She passed it on to Alan, who had already begun to write songs while in Georgia, and he was soon signed up with Campbell's company. Later, he became one of the first country acts under contract to Arista Records.

Alan's string of consecutive Number 1 songs includes 'Here In The Real World' and 'Don't Rock The Jukebox.' The latter was *Billboard*'s top country single of the year for 1991 and ASCAP's Country Song of the Year for 1992.

Jackson's first album, *Here In The Real World*, containing the title song and four other hits, was certified platinum. His second album, *Don't Rock The Jukebox*, also featuring the title song and four other singles, went double platinum; while his third album, *A Lot About Livin' (And A Little 'Bout Love)*, on which he wrote or co-wrote seven of the ten cuts including 'Tonight I Climbed The Wall' and 'Chattahoochee', has also gone platinum.

SONNY JAMES

Sonny James began his career at the age of 4 while singing with his family. By the time he was a teenager, he had his own Birmingham, Alabama radio show.

Born James Loden in Hackleburg, Alabama on May 1, 1929, Sonny continued his career during the Fifties while he was in the military, serving in Korea.

The singer/songwriter/guitarist/producer had his first hit record, 'That's Me Without You,' in 1953. Sonny's 1956 recording of 'Young Love' became both his first Number 1 pop and country single and his signature song.

Known as "the Southern Gentleman," Sonny, together with his band the Southern Gentlemen, had an unprecedented unbroken string of 16 Number 1 records from 1967 through 1971, including 'Need You,' 'Heaven Says Hello' and 'Here Comes Honey Again'.

WAYLON JENNINGS

Waylon Arnold Jennings was born on June 15, 1937 in Littlefield, Texas.

At the age of 12, Waylon had his own local radio show. By 1957 he had moved to Lubbock, Texas where he became a disc jockey before joining Buddy Holly as bass player until Buddy's death in 1959.

In 1960, Waymore, as he came to be known, moved to Phoenix, Arizona, forming his own group, the Waylors. He began making records in 1961 but it wasn't until he moved to Nashville in 1975 that he had his first hits. During the late Sixties and early Seventies Waylon had such successes as 'Only Daddy That'll Walk The Line,' 'Yours Love' and 'The Taker.'

By 1975 Jennings was recording duets with Willie Nelson who, along with Tompall Glaser and Jennings' wife, Jessi Colter (recording individually and as a quartet) were by then being dubbed "The Outlaws" of country music. Ten years later Jennings, Nelson, Johnny Cash and Kris Kristofferson were recording and touring as "The Highwaymen."

Throughout Jennings' solo career he has recorded with others including Anita Carter, Jerry Reed and Hank Williams, Jr.

In 1993, Waylon turned to recording country music for children, releasing on May 25, on the Ode 2 Kids label, an LP titled *Cowboys, Sisters, Rascals And Dirt*.

GEORGE JONES

See separate entry in the Legends section.

KRIS KRISTOFFERSON

When Kris Kristofferson moved to Nashville in 1965, he became one of country's first singer/songwriters.

Named for his father, a career military man, Kris Kristofferson was born on June 22, 1936 in Brownsville, Texas. The family moved to San Mateo, California when Kris was in high school. While attending Pomona College in California, he accepted a Rhodes scholarship and moved to England to study literature at Oxford University from 1958 through 1959. While in England, Kris was writing songs and once he received his Oxford degree began to perform using the name Kris Carson.

Kris then enlisted with every intention of making the service his career, but when his songs were received enthusiastically at the NCO clubs, he was persuaded to send his material to Nashville.

Nashville publisher Marijohn Wilkin was so impressed with Kris's work that Kristofferson, who was having second thoughts about his career

Kris Kristofferson—the Rhodes scholar whose erudite lyrics have attracted many converts to country music.

path, moved to Nashville once his tour was up, taking a mundane day job emptying the ash trays at Columbia Records' offices.

Kristofferson's early songs were recorded by Roy Drusky, Ray Stevens, Faron Young, Ray Price and Kristofferson's mentor, Johnny Cash, leading to Kris securing a recording contract of his own.

Kris had a Number 1 country hit (Number 16 on the pop charts) with a song he co-wrote with Marijohn Wilkin, 'Why Me.' Kristofferson's début album, *Kristofferson*, features the composer's own versions of songs popularized by others, including 'Me And Bobby McGee,' 'Help Me Make It Through The Night' and 'For The Good Times.'

k. d. lang

Katherine Dawn Lang was born on November 2, 1961 in Consort, Alberta, Canada.

k.d. (the lower-case spelling of her name is the singer's own affectation) grew up revering the music of Patsy Cline. Later she paid Patsy the ultimate tribute by dubbing her own band the ReClines.

The Canadian Country Music Association's Entertainer of the Year in 1987, lang first received recognition at the age of 22 when her first album, *A Truly Western Experience*, was released in Canada in 1984. By the age of 25 lang had released an album in America, 1987's *Angel With A Lariat*.

Kitty Wells and Brenda Lee. In 1989 k.d. received another Grammy (Best Country Vocal Performance, Female) for her album *Absolute Torch And Twang*.

In 1993, k.d. won Grammys for *Ingenue* and 'Constant Craving' and also won three Juno awards in her native Canada (for Album, Producer and Songwriter of the Year).

LITTLE TEXAS

Individually they are Tim Rushlow (lead singer), Duane Propes (bassist/vocalist), Del Gray (drummer), Brady Seals (keyboardist/vocalist) and guitarist/vocalists Porter Howell and Dwayne O'Brien. Collectively, they are the band known as Little Texas.

The group's 1992 début CD *First Time For Everything* spawned four Top 10 singles including the title cut, their début single, 1991's 'Some Guys Have All The Love,' 'You And Forever And Me,' and 'I'd Rather Miss You.'

Little Texas's inception dates back to 1984 when Rushlow and O'Brien first began to perform as a duo in Arlington, Texas. In 1988 Tim and Dwayne hooked with Duane and Porter (of Longview, Texas), eventually completing the group with Ohio natives Del and Brady (Brady is veteran country singer Dan Seals's cousin).

The sextet's oxymoronic name comes not from the Lone Star state origins of some of its young members— all of whom are still in their twenties—but from a community located 35 miles south of Nashville.

k. d. lang—country's only acknowledged lesbian—has yet to win over American radio.

The singer won her first Grammy in 1988 (for Best Country Vocal Collaboration) when she and Roy Orbison were recognized for their remake of Orbison's 1961 pop hit, 'Crying.'

In 1988, k.d. also recorded Shadowland, noted for the medley 'Honky Tonk Angels' featuring Loretta Lynn,

THE LOUVIN BROTHERS

Alabama farm boys Lonnie Ira (born April 21, 1924) and Charlie Elzer (born July 7, 1927) Loudermilk began their country music careers working in Chattanooga with the Foggy Mountain Boys in 1943.

Ira went on to join Charlie Monroe's Kentucky Partners in the mid Forties, while both brothers took the stage name Louvin in 1947 when, as the Louvin Brothers, they worked at Knoxville's WROL Radio.

The Louvin Brothers began recording for Decca Records in 1949, before moving on to Capitol Records in 1952 where their 1955 hit 'When I Stop Dreaming' brought them an invitation to join the Grand Ole Opry. The Louvins were regulars at the Opry for 2 years before returning in 1959.

In 1963, following a string of hits from 1955 through 1962 including 'I Don't Believe You've Met My Baby,' 'You're Running Wild' and 'My Baby's Gone,' the Louvins disbanded. On June 28, 1965, Ira Louvin was killed in an automobile accident.

Remaining with the Opry following Ira's death, Charlie continued to make records (Charlie's 'I Don't Love You Anymore' and 'See The Big Man Cry' were hits for him while Ira was still alive) on his own and with Emmylou Harris ('Love Don't Care', released in 1979), Jim And Jesse ('North Wind,' released in 1982) and Melba Montgomery (six singles from 1970 through 1973). Charlie continues to make some 200 personal appearances each year. The owner/operator of the Louvin Brothers Music Park in his hometown of Henager, Alabama, Charlie hosts bluegrass and country-music festivals three times a year.

LYLE LOVETT

Lyle Lovett was born in Klein, Texas on November 1, 1957. He began writing songs while attending Texas' A and M University, where he received degrees in journalism (1980) and German (1981).

After playing clubs in several Texas cities, Lovett journeyed to Europe where he performed at the Schueberover Annual Fair in Luxembourg. Returning to the States, Lyle made a demo tape and headed for Nashville, pitching the tape to a fellow Texan, ASCAP executive Merlin Littlefield. Littlefield liked Lovett's songs and before long Lovett had both a writer's contract with a music publisher and, by 1986, a record deal with MCA/Curb. His early hits included 'Cowboy Man,' 'Why I Don't Know,' and 'She's No Lady.'

Lyle won a 1989 Grammy (Best Country Vocal Performance, Male) for his album *Lyle Lovett and his Large Band*.

He has been featured in two Robert Altman films: *The Player* and *Short Cuts* and his music, along with that of Nanci Griffiths, is included in the soundtrack of *The Firm*, a 1993 movie starring Tom Cruise.

Loretta Lynn

See separate entry in the Legends section.

Reba McEntire

Reba Nell McEntire was born in McAlester, Oklahoma on March 28, 1955.

As a teenager, she sang with her older brother Pake (later with RCA) and younger sister Susie (now a Christian music singer). Known as the Singing McEntires, the siblings performed at rodeos, where Reba also competed as a horseback barrel rider.

Red Steagall discovered Reba in 1974 when McEntire sang the 'The Star-Spangled Banner' at the National Rodeo Finals in Oklahoma City, Oklahoma. McEntire, who had Top 20 and Top 30 country duets with Jacky Ward in 1979, had a Top 10 duet in 1991 when she and Vince Gill recorded 'Oklahoma Swing' and again in 1993 when she and Vince released 'The Heart Won't Lie.'

A Grand Ole Opry member since 1985, Reba was the Country Music Association's 1986 Entertainer of the Year. She has platinum, double platinum and gold albums to her credit. Her many Number 1 hits include 'Who-ever's In New England,' (which won McEntire a 1986 Grammy for Best Country Vocal Performance, Female), 'Little Rock' and 'The Last One To Know.'

Reba McEntire continues to take country music to new heights.

BARBARA MANDRELL

Barbara Ann Mandrell was born on December 25, 1948. Raised in Oceanside, California, where her grade school classmates nicknamed her Barbed Wire, Barbara played in a family band.

At age 10, Mandrell was playing pedal steel guitar and saxophone on a Bakersfield, California radio show. At 11 she was performing in Las Vegas with Joe and Rose Lee Maphis and appeared on Compton, California's *Town Hall Party* TV series.

At 13 she toured with Johnny Cash, Patsy Cline and George Jones. Mandrell appeared on ABC TV's *Five Star Jubilee* TV show during the Sixties, making her first record for a small label in 1963.

Barbara's first chart record was released in 1969 when she moved to Nashville and began to have a series of hits through the Eighties including 'Sleeping Single In A Double Bed,' 'Years' and 'I Was Country When Country Wasn't Cool' (featuring George Jones). Her duet partners have included David Houston, the Oak Ridge Boys and Lee Greenwood (Waylon Jennings sang on Barbara's 1988 recording 'Angels Love Bad Men').

Barbara, Louise and Irlene Mandrell hosted *Barbara Mandrell and the Mandrell Sisters*, an NBC TV weekly variety series from 1980 through 1982. The series later re-ran on The Nashville Network (TNN).

In 1984, when Barbara was seriously injured in a head-on collision, the singer received the largest single deliv-

Barbara Mandrell was certifiably country when country wasn't cool.

ery of mail to any Nashvillian ever! A two-time Grammy winner, Mandrell has also been twice named the CMA Entertainer of the Year (1980 and 1981).

Her autobiography, *Get to the Heart: My Story*, was published in 1990.

ROGER MILLER

Roger Dean Miller was born on January 2, 1936 in Fort Worth, Texas.

Raised in Erick, Oklahoma, Miller moved to Nashville in the mid Fifties and began his songwriting career, taking jobs as a sideman for Faron Young, Ray Price, Patsy Cline and Johnny Cash.

In 1960, Roger had his first country hit, 'You Don't Want My Love'. Formerly Faron Young's drummer, Roger was enjoying pop and country success by 1964 when he had hits with 'Dang Me,' 'Chug-A-Lug' and, the next year, with his signature song 'King Of The Road'.

Miller won five Grammy Awards in 1964 and swept the ceremonies again the following year winning an unprecedented six Grammys, leading to a short-lived 1966 NBC-TV musical variety series, *The Roger Miller Show*.

Roger continued to have hit records during the Seventies and Eighties, winning five gold albums, five gold singles and induction into the Nashville Songwriters Hall of Fame.

By the mid Eighties Miller's interest had turned to stage plays and in 1985 Roger received a Tony Award for scoring the Broadway musical 'Big River', adapted from Mark Twain's *The Adventures of Huckleberry Finn*.

Roger was later diagnosed as having lung cancer and died in Los Angeles soon afterwards on October 25, 1992. Today, Roger Dean Miller Jr carries on his father's musical tradition.

RONNIE MILSAP

When Ronnie Millsaps (the singer's real name) was born on January 16, 1943 in Robbinsville, North Carolina he had only "light vision."

At the age of 6, Ronnie was sent to the North Carolina State School for the Blind where his musical aptitude surfaced. By the age of 12 Ronnie had learned to play several instruments.

Milsap worked with several bands and with J. J. Cale before moving first to Memphis, making a name for himself there, and then to Nashville. Ronnie's first country hit, 'I Hate You,' was released in 1973. Since then he has had over 40 Number 1 records including 'Pure Love,' 'My Heart' and 'Show Her.' Milsap's duet partners have included Kenny Rogers and Mike Reid.

A six-time Grammy winner, a Grand Ole Opry member since 1976 and the Country Music Association's 1977 Entertainer of the Year, Milsap has sold over 20 million records.

A ham radio operator, Ronnie built the first 48-track studio on Music Row.

Milsap's autobiography, *Almost Like A Song* (the title of one of his hits), was published in 1990.

BILL MONROE

Bill Monroe, the Father of Bluegrass Music, was born on September 13, 1911 in Rosine, Kentucky, the youngest of four children. Left an orphan, Bill went to live with his Uncle Pen Vandiver, the same fiddler Ricky Skaggs pays tribute to in his 1984 hit, 'Uncle Pen.' Beginning his career as one of the Monroe Brothers, a trio which also included Bill's siblings Birch and Charlie, Bill performed on radio stations in Indiana before touring with Chicago's WLS *National Barn Dance* road show during the early Thirties.

When Birch found work at a refinery, he dropped out of the group, leaving Bill and Charlie as a duo, with Charlie singing lead. It wasn't long until Charlie and Bill had a recording contract. But each brother was strong-willed and an unresolved personality conflict resulted in the brothers' professional break-up in 1938.

Bill joined the Grand Ole Opry in 1939. He was inducted into the Country Music Hall of Fame in 1970 and in 1993 he received a Grammy Lifetime Achievement Award.

Bill Monroe, as well as being a Country Music Hall of Famer is also the recipient of a Grammy Lifetime Achievement Award.

PATSY MONTANA

Ruby (later spelt Rubye) Blevins (Patsy Montana), an Arkansas native, was born on October 30, 1912. A fiddle player, known for her yodeling, Patsy popularized songs such as 'I'm An Old Cowhand' and 'Singing In Saddle.'

On August 16, 1935, while a member of a western swing-influenced group called the Prairie Ramblers, Montana recorded 'I Want To Be A Cowboy's

Sweetheart.' Patsy's signature song, this was the first country gold record ever recorded by a woman.

GEORGE MORGAN

George Morgan is remembered by his fellow Grand Ole Opry artists as quite a practical joker. One gag involved George's pretending to be depressed. The set-up involved luring a concerned friend to Morgan's hotel room where he found George face down in a bathtub covered with blood (the blood was actually ketchup).

Born in Waverly, Tennessee on June 28, 1924, and raised in Barberton, Ohio, Morgan began his career during the late Forties at WWVA's *Wheeling Jamboree*.

George's first charted country recording of 'Candy Kisses' (which he wrote) became his signature song and was a Number 1 record for him in 1949. His other hits included 'Room Full Of Roses,' 'Almost' and 'Slippin' Around,' a duet with fellow Opry star Marion Worth.

George joined the Grand Ole Opry in 1948, leaving in 1956 when he hosted his own local television show in Nashville on WLAC TV (now WTVF). The series ran until 1959, in which year George returned to the Opry. He remained in the Opry until his death on July 7, 1975 following complications arising from heart surgery.

LORRIE MORGAN

Lorrie Morgan is one of country music's few native Nashvillians. Born in Music City, USA on June 27, 1959, Loretta Lynn Morgan was the fifth and youngest child of George and Anna Morgan.

When she was 13, Lorrie first sang on the Grand Ole Opry (she became a member at the age of 24). One of her earliest charting recordings, 'I'm Completely Satisfied With You,' was an electronically produced "duet" with her late father.

Shortly after Morgan had her first releases for RCA Records ('Trainwreck of Emotion,' a Top 20 hit followed by Lorrie's signature song, 'Dear Me,' a Top 10 record) she was widowed when her second husband, Keith Whitley, died suddenly on May 9, 1989. Prior to Keith's death, Morgan had recorded duets with Whitley including the Grammy-nominated 'When A Tear Becomes A Rose' (Lorrie prefers the others not be released).

Morgan's platinum albums include her début effort on RCA, *Leave The Light On* and *Something In Red* (Lorrie's third album, *Watch Me*, went gold).

Morgan has had several Number 1 hits including 'Five Minutes,' 'Watch Me,' 'What Part Of No' and 'I Guess You Had To Be There.'

WILLIE NELSON

A native of Abbott, Texas, Willie Hugh Nelson was born on April 30, 1933.

He learned to play guitar at the age of 10. After serving in the Air Force during the Korean conflict, Nelson worked as a disc jockey in Waco, San Antonio, and Houston, Texas, before becoming bass player to Ray Price.

Nelson moved to Nashville in 1960, writing songs recorded by Patsy Cline ('Crazy'), Ray Price ('Night Life'), Faron Young ('Night Life') and Billy Walker ('Funny How Time Slips Away').

Willie's many Number 1 hit recordings include his signature song, 'On The Road Again,' 'Always On My Mind,' and 'Living In The Promiseland.'

Nelson has sung with Ray Charles, Hank Cochran, David Allan Coe, Shirley Collie, Merle Haggard, Julio Iglesias, Brenda Lee, Darrell McCall, Tracy Nelson, Dolly Parton, Marky Kay Place, Ray Price, Roy Rogers, Leon Russell, Sinead O'Connor, Bob Dylan, David Crosby and Paul Simon (in addition to his Highwaymen colleagues).

The "Red-Headed Stranger" (Willie's nickname and the autobiographical title of his classic recording and hit feature film) returned to Texas in 1970 where he hosted the first of his annual Fourth of July picnic concerts in 1972 in Austin.

There Willie is acknowledged as one of the creator's of country music's "Austin sound" and, along with his

Willie Nelson was recognized as a songwriter years before being accepted as a singer.

new singing partner, Waylon Jennings, one of country's "outlaws."

The Country Music Association's 1979 Entertainer of the Year is now the president of Farm Aid Inc., an ongoing effort, through Nelson's annual concert/telethon, to raise both awareness and money to aid the plight of America's family farmers.

Willie: An Autobiography was published in 1988.

THE NITTY GRITTY DIRT BAND

Originally a duet of Jeff Hanna and Bruce Kunkel which grew into a sextet known as the Illegitimate Jug Band when it formed in 1966, the Nitty Gritty Dirt Band (following several additions and deletions of personnel, including Jackson Browne) has pared down to a quartet.

Its current members are vocalists Jeff Hanna (guitar), Jimmie Fadden (drums and harmonica), Jimmy Ibbotson (bass, mandolin and guitar) and Bob Carpenter (keyboards and accordion).

Hadden, Fadden, John McEuen, Ralph Barr, Leslie Thompson and Bruce Kunkel were the NGDB's founding members.

In 1972 the group produced its historic album, *Will The Circle Be Unbroken*, and, in 1989, *Will The Circle Be Unbroken: Volume Two*.

Known simply as the Dirt Band after Hanna left in 1976, the members reverted to calling themselves the Nitty Gritty Dirt Band in 1982.

The NGDB's hits include its signature song, 'Mr. Bojangles,' 'Modern Day Romance' and 'Fishin' In The Dark.'

THE OAK RIDGE BOYS

Today's Oak Ridge Boys inherited their name from the original Oak Ridge Quartet, a Tennessee-based country-turned-gospel group formed in 1945. The present quartet consists of lead singer Duane Allen (born April 29, 1943 in Taylortown, Texas), bass singer Richard Sterban (born April 24, 1943 in Camden, New Jersey), tenor Joe Bonsall (born May 18, 1948 in Philadelphia, Pennsylvania) and baritone Steve Sanders, formerly the ORB's rhythm guitarist, who replaced the Oaks' longtime baritone William Lee Golden in 1987 (born September 17, 1952 in Richland, Georgia).

Easing their way out of gospel during the mid Seventies, the Mighty Oaks, as the group is nicknamed, had its first Top 5 record as a country group in 1977 with 'Y'all Come Back Saloon.'

The Oaks' first charting country record 'Praise The Lord (And Pass The Soup)' in 1977 featured Johnny Cash and the Carter Family. In 1986 the ORB recorded 'When You Get To The Heart', a Top 20 hit, with Barbara Mandrell.

The Oaks' Number 1 singles include their signature song, 'Elvira,' 'Bobbie Sue,' and 'Gonna Take A Lot Of River.'

KAY T. OSLIN

Kay Toinette Oslin was born on May 15, 1942 in Crossitt, Arkansas and raised in Mobile, Alabama and in Houston, Texas. In Houston in the Sixties, Oslin was in a folk trio before moving to New York City where, as a stage actress, she appeared in musicals such as *West Side Story*, *Hello Dolly* and *Promises*, and in TV commercials.

A budding country singer/songwriter, Kay T. Oslin, as she was billed in 1981, released a single that charted, but real success in country music eluded her until shortly after she moved to Nashville in 1985. Borrowing money from her aunt, Oslin financed a showcase which brought her to the attention of RCA Records. Once signed to RCA, Oslin proved that a woman past 40 could still become an "overnight" country star.

K.T.'s first RCA release, in 1987, was a Top 40 country record, but it was Oslin's second single that year, 'Eighties Ladies,' that made her a star. Oslin's platinum-selling *Eighties Ladies* album, featuring the title cut, débuted at Number 15, the highest position ever for a female artist.

In 1987, 'Eighties Ladies' brought Oslin her first Grammy for Best Country Vocal Performance, Female. The Country Music Association's 1988 Female Vocalist of the Year, K.T. also received the CMA's Song of the Year honors for 'Eighties Ladies' as well as two more Grammys for her follow-up hit and third Number 1 record, 'Hold Me,' following 'Do Ya' and 'I'll Always Come Back.'

MARIE OSMOND

Olive Marie Osmond was born in Ogden, Utah on October 13, 1959.

The only girl in a family of eight boys (including the six performing sons), Marie made her singing début at the age of 3.

Osmond established herself as a country star in 1973 when she covered Anita Bryant's 1960 pop hit, 'Paper Roses.' Produced by Sonny James, Marie's version of 'Paper Roses' was a gold record. Number 1 on the country charts, 'Paper Roses' peaked at Number 5 on the pop charts.

At 14 Marie began performing in concert with her famous rock 'n' rolling brothers who were international teen idols.

Marie's second crossover hit, in 1974, was a duet with her brother Donny, 'I'm Leaving It Up To You' (a remake of Dale and Grace's 1963 pop classic).

The pairing of Donny and Marie proved so popular that they starred in their own ABC-TV musical variety series from 1976 through 1979. Each week the duo performed a medley, one of the more popular segments of the show, in which Marie identified herself as being "a little bit country" while Donny insisted he was "a little bit rock 'n' roll."

When *The Donny and Marie Show* ended, Marie resumed her country music career, but it wasn't until she cut a duet with Dan Seals, in 1985, that she topped the country charts again. 'Meet Me In Montana' was a Number 1 hit for Osmond and Seals. Marie's follow-up solo effort produced another Number 1 song for her in 1985: 'There's No Stopping Your Heart.'

Her next Number 1 came in 1986 when she and Paul Davis recorded 'You're Still New To Me.' That duet pairing was such a success that, in 1988, Marie and Paul released a remake of Davis' 1978 solo pop hit, 'Sweet Life.'

Marie, who MCs the annual Children's Miracle Network Telethon to benefit children's hospitals, received the Roy Acuff Community Service Award in 1988.

Marie Osmond: the only Osmond to be "a little bit country."

PAUL OVERSTREET

Paul Overstreet was born in Newton, Mississippi on March 17, 1955.

Raised in Van Cleave, Mississippi, Paul began writing songs while he was still a child.

Overstreet came to Nashville in 1973 to become a country star. When his plans didn't immediately materialize, he took a job in Nashville's famed Printer's Alley downtown nightclub district, working two nights a week for $25 a night.

Paul also spent 5 years on the road with a variety of bands, playing bass, drums and guitar until he got burnt out in the late Seventies.

By 1980 Overstreet had landed a recording contract with RCA Records but left the label when his efforts there proved unsuccessful.

Paul's first big break as a songwriter came in 1983 when George Jones had a Top 10 record on Overstreet's 'Same Ole Me.'

As a singer, Overstreet broke through in 1987, when he wrote and recorded his first hit with Tanya Tucker and Paul Davis. The song 'I Won't Take Less Than Your Love' was a Number 1 country record.

Also during the mid Eighties Paul signed with MTM Records as a member of a recording trio including fellow songwriters Thom Schuyler and Fred Knobloch. Schuyler, Knobloch And Overstreet (SKO for short) had three hits including 'Baby's Got A New Baby,' which became a Number 1 record, before Paul chose to leave the act in order to re-establish his solo career.

As a solo act, Overstreet recorded 'Love Helps Those (Who Cannot Help Themselves)' for the now-defunct MTM. That recording peaked at Number 3 on the country charts.

When MTM folded, Paul returned to RCA, where there has been renewed interest in Overstreet's career as a singer largely on the strength of his songwriting. He has written or co-written such songs as 'Forever And Ever Amen,' 'On The Other Hand,' 'Diggin' Up Bones,' 'No Place Like Home,' and 'Deeper Than The Holler' (all hits for Randy Travis), 'When You Say Nothing At All' (Keith Whitley), 'You're Still New To Me' (Marie Osmond and Paul Davis), 'One Love At A Time' (Tanya Tucker), 'Long Line Of Love' (Michael Martin Murphey), 'I Fell In Love Again Last Night' and 'You Again' (the Forester Sisters).

Overstreet's own recordings, such as 'Daddy's Come Around (To Mama's Way Of Thinkin'),' 'All The Fun,' and 'Seein' My Father in Me' stress themes of fidelity and love of family, subjects in which Paul is well-versed.

A "preacher's kid" whose parents divorced when Overstreet was 5, Paul is a family man. As of 1993 he and his wife Julie are the parents of five small children.

✪ ✪ ✪

BUCK OWENS

Alvis Edgar Owens, Jr was born in Sherman, Texas on August 12, 1929.

Raised in Mesa, Arizona, in 1951 Buck moved to Bakersfield, California (where he would be one of the originators of the Bakersfield Sound), playing trumpet and saxophone with his band, the Schoolhouse Playboys. Also at this time he worked sessions with such artists as Faron Young, Wanda Jackson and Sonny James.

In 1955 Buck began his career recording rockabilly using the name Corky Jones (his 1988 recording of 'Hot Dog' was actually a remake of a song he first recorded under the Jones stage name in 1956). He reverted to his own name when he charted with his first Capitol single in 1959. Since then, Buck has had over 20 Number 1 records, including 'Act Naturally' (covered by the Beatles), 'Together Again' and 'Tall Dark Stranger.' Buck owes much of his success to his bands: the award-winning Buckaroo band (featuring the late great Don Rich) and the Bakersfield Brass band.

His duet partners have included his son Buddy Alan, Emmylou Harris, Rose Maddox, Susan Raye and Dwight Yoakam. On TV Owens hosted the syndicated Buck Owens Ranch Show before co-hosting (with Roy Clark) Hee-Haw from 1969 through 1986. Today Buck is more or less semi-retired from country music and spends most of his time overseeing his many business interests (such as his own radio stations and "shopper" newspapers).

DOLLY PARTON

Dolly Rebecca Parton was born on January 19, 1946 in Sevier County, Tennessee.

A Knoxville, Tennessee radio performer and recording artist by the age of 11 (at 13 Parton was able to perform an extra song when she made a guest appearance on the Grand Ole Opry, thanks to the graciousness of Jimmy C. Newman, who hosted the portion of the show on which she appeared), Dolly began to pursue her career in earnest in 1964 after she graduated from high school and moved to Nashville the very next day.

Porter Wagoner gave Dolly her first big break, making her a part of his syndicated TV show in 1967. (Parton would later have both a syndicated and a network TV series bearing her name.) Dolly toured and recorded with Porter from 1967 until she left his organization in 1974.

Parton joined the Grand Ole Opry in 1969. Dolly wrote and recorded over 20 Number 1 hits in the years that followed, including 'Jolene,' 'I Will Always Love You' and '9 To 5.'

Dolly's feature film credits include *Nine to Five, The Best Little Whorehouse in Texas, Rhinestone, Wild Texas Wind, Steel Magnolias* and *Straight Talk* (Parton has a star on the Hollywood Walk of Fame).

Dolly Parton quickly became the blue-collar country fan's idea of a sex symbol.

Dolly counts Porter Wagoner, Willie Nelson, Kenny Rogers, Linda Ronstadt, Emmylou Harris, Tanya Tucker, Kathy Mattea, Mary-Chapin Carpenter, Loretta Lynn, Tammy Wynette, Ricky Van Shelton, Pam Tillis, Billy Ray Cyrus, Collin Raye and Billy Dean among her singing partners.

With three platinum and four gold-selling albums to her credit, Parton, the Country Music Association's 1978 Entertainer of the Year, is the first recipient of the CMA's Country Music Honors (1993).

Dolly's theme park, Dollywood, has attracted tourists to Pigeon Forge, Tennessee since 1987. In 1988 Parton established the Dollywood Foundation for continuing education.

The American Academy of Achievement has honored Parton and her worldwide success by awarding Dolly its Gold Plate Award in 1992 and inducting country music's cultural icon into its Museum of Living History.

JOHNNY PAYCHECK

His name was Donald Eugene Lytle when he was born on May 31, 1941 in Greenfield, Ohio.

After the singer/guitarist/steel guitarist moved to Nashville in 1959, Lytle, who had worked with Faron Young, Ray Price, Porter Wagoner and George Jones, changed his name to Donnie Young. Still using his given name when he first recorded for Decca in the early Sixties, Lytle decided on the name change, taking it a step further in 1965 when he became Johnny Paycheck (taking the name of a small-time heavyweight boxer whom Joe Louis knocked out in two rounds back in 1940).

Paycheck recorded his own first Top 10 country single in 1966. In the same year two more of his songs became hits when they were recorded by Ray Price ('Touch My Heart') and Tammy Wynette ('Apartment #9'). Johnny's career got sidetracked when he began passing bad checks and ended up behind bars, but during the early Seventies he got back on track again with hits like 'She's All I Got,' 'Someone To Give My Love To' and 'Mr Lovemaker.'

During the Seventies "outlaw" period in country music Paycheck altered his name again, becoming John Austin Paycheck, but he had no hits under that name. Johnny's only Number 1 hit came in 1977 when he recorded his signature song, the working man's anthem 'Take This Job And Shove It,' written by David Allan Coe.

Johnny recorded his last hit in 1980 and then spent the latter part of the following decade back in prison. In the Nineties, he has been paroled.

MINNIE PEARL

See separate entry in the Legends section.

WEBB PIERCE

Webb Pierce was born in West Monroe, Louisiana on August 8, 1926.

Pierce went from Monroe radio station KMLB to the *Louisiana Hayride* where he performed during the early Fifties through to 1955. Having moved to Nashville, he continued a string of hits that began in 1952 when he recorded three consecutive Number 1 records for Decca: 'Wondering,' 'That Heart Belongs To Me' and 'Back Street Affair.' Webb's band then included such up-and-comers as Faron Young and Floyd Cramer.

Though Pierce had hits through 1964 and duet partners including Mel Tillis, Willie Nelson, Kitty Wells and Red Sovine, the Fifties were really the decade when he dominated the charts, scoring such successes as 'There Stands The Glass' (a classic drinking song banned by many radio stations), 'Slowly' and 'More And More.'

Known for his flamboyance (he owned, for example, a coin-studded car), Pierce ran into trouble with his neighbor Ray Stevens during the Seventies when Stevens objected to the presence of tour buses converging on his neighborhood at Pierce's invitation to view the latter's guitar-shaped swimming pool. Eventually Pierce relented and the pool was moved to a park area of Music Row.

A co-owner of Nashville's Cedarwood music publishing company, Webb was also a film star with *Buffalo Guns*, *Music City, USA*, and *Road to Nashville* among his credits. Webb Pierce died on February 24, 1991.

RAY PRICE

Ray Noble Price was born in Perryville, Texas on January 12, 1926.

Raised in Dallas, Price was attending North Texas Agricultural College in Abilene, Texas before he was drafted into the Marines, serving from 1944 to 1946. A protégé of Hank Williams (and Hank's one-time roommate), Price left school again in 1948 to work on Abilene's KRBC Radio's *Hillbilly Circus*, moving on to Dallas' *Big D Jamboree* and, in 1952, the Grand Ole Opry.

Known as "The Cherokee Cowboy" for his birthplace—Cherokee County, Texas—Price named his band (which included Buddy Emmons, Roger Miller, Johnny Paycheck, Willie Nelson, Darrell McCall and Johnny Bush) the Cherokee Cowboys, and began his recording career on the Bullet label in 1950. Success came only after moving on to Columbia Records in 1952, where he had such hits as 'Crazy Arms,' 'City Lights' and 'For The Good Times' during his 22 years with the label. (Price has also recorded nearly 55 albums.)

Ray won a Grammy (Best Country Vocal Performance, Male) in 1970 for 'For The Good Times' and the Country Music Association's 1971 Album of the Year Award for *I Won't Mention It Again*.

He plays 150 dates each year.

CHARLEY PRIDE

Charley Frank Pride was born on March 18, 1938 in Sledge, Mississippi.

He began life as professional baseball player, playing for the Negro American League's Memphis Red Sox from 1954 through 1956. After military service from 1956 through 1958, he moved to Montana, working as a zinc smelter and playing semi-pro baseball in the Pioneer Leagues. Hewas one of baseball's California Angels for about 2 weeks in 1961, before being advised he was not major league material. In 1962, while negotiating with the New York Mets, he broke his ankle during an accident at the smelter.

Having begun to sing in local clubs about 1960, his first music career break came in 1963 when he was discovered by Red Sovine. Sovine urged Charley to come to Nashville. By 1966, country music's most successful black performer was signed to RCA Records where he had seven Top 10 releases (following 'Snakes Crawl At Night') between 1966 and 1969. These were followed by six consecutive Number 1 records including 'All I Have To Offer You (Is Me),' 'Is Anybody Goin' To San Antone,' and 'I'd Rather Love You.'

Pride, the Country Music Association's 1971 Entertainer of the Year, is a three-time Grammy award-winner. With 36 Number 1 singles, 12 gold LPs in the United States and four platinum records internationally, Charley was inducted into the Grand Ole Opry in 1993.

JIM REEVES

James Travis Reeves was born in Panola County, Texas on August 20, 1924.

Although he could play guitar by the time he was 10, Reeves wanted to play professional baseball and had actually signed to play St Louis Cardinals' farm team when a broken ankle forced him to abandoned his plans.

A disc jockey at KWKH Radio in Shreveport, Louisiana, Jim joined the *Louisiana Hayride* following his first country hit, 'Mexican Joe,' a Number 1 single for Reeves and the Circle O Ranch Boys in 1953. Jim's follow-up record, 'Bimbo,' was also a Number 1 hit. 'Bimbo' sold 600,000 copies and made the Top 30 of the pop charts.

In 1955 Reeves joined the Grand Ole Opry, continuing to have Number 1 country hits which also crossed over, including 'Four Walls' (1957) and 'He'll Have To Go' (1959). Jim starred in the 1963 South African film *Kimberly Jim*.

Though Gentleman Jim, as Reeves was known, died in a plane crash on July 31, 1964, his records continued to chart through 1980 and are still selling, thanks to electronic reproduction, the marketing savvy of Reeves' widow, Mary, and the wealth of recorded material Jim left behind.

Reeves and Dottie West's recording of 'Love Is No Excuse' peaked at Number 7 on the country charts following its March 28, 1964 début. Posthumously, Jim and

Patsy Cline were paired ('Have You Ever Been Lonely' was released in 1981, 'I Fall To Pieces' in 1982) followed by a creative 1983 release, *The Jim Reeves Medley*, featuring 'Four Walls,' 'I Missed Me,' 'He'll Have To Go,' and 'Oh, How I Miss You, Tonight.' But the most bizarre pairing was a series of

Reeves' music remains so popular worldwide that younger listeners, not realizing Jim died three decades ago, still ask about his touring schedule.

three Top 10 singles released during 1979 and 1980, all "duets" by Jim and Deborah Allen. Allen was 11 years old at the time of Jim's death and had never met him.

Jim Reeves was posthumously inducted into the Country Music Hall of Fame in 1967.

JEANNIE C. RILEY

Jeannie Carolyn Stephenson was born in Anson, Texas on October 19, 1944 and began singing when she was a high school sophomore. A couple of years later, she married Mickey Riley and had a child, Kim, in 1966 before heading to Nashville where she pitched her demo tapes for 2 years. Making music industry contacts such as Johnny Russell and the Wilburn Brothers along the way (she had an early opportunity to open shows for Johnny Paycheck in Las Vegas), Jeannie took a day job as music publisher/songwriter Jerry Chesnut's secretary. By 1968 the singing secretary was a Plantation Records artist, releasing in August of that year 'Harper Valley P.T.A.'

Written by Tom T. Hall and passed on by Skeeter Davis and Jean Shepard, Jeannie reluctantly recorded the song, but was glad she did when it not only became a Number 1 pop and country hit, but a gold record as well, selling five million copies worldwide within 4 months of its release. 'Harper Valley P.T.A.' became Riley's signature song, garnering her a Grammy in 1968 and a CMA Award that same year.

Though she had several other hits during the Sixties and Seventies, including 'The Girl Most Likely,' 'There Never Was A Time' and 'Good Enough To Be Your Wife,' 'Harper Valley P.T.A.' remains Jeannie's most-requested song.

Riley published her autobiography, *From Harper Valley to the Mountaintop*, in 1981, recording a duet album with Tommy Cash on Playback Records a decade later.

TEX RITTER

Maurice Woodward Ritter was born near Murvaul, Texas on January 12, 1905.

While attending the University of Texas at Austin, he became interested in authentic cowboy songs. He began his singing career in 1929 at Houston's KRPC Radio and then spent 2 years at Northwestern University Law School near Chicago before leaving to pursue a Broadway career, starring in a handful of stage plays, including *Green Grow the Lilacs* in 1931, and acquiring his nickname in the process.

During the early Thirties, Tex starred in a series called *Cowboy Tom's Roundup* and hosted New York's WHN *Barn Dance*. By 1936 he had moved to Hollywood, where he became one of the most popular singing cowboy film stars of the Thirties and Forties.

Having begun his recording career in 1933, Ritter had his first Number 1 in 1944 with 'I'm Wastin' My Tears Over You.' It was followed by such hits as 'Jealous Heart' 'High Noon' (the title song from the soundtrack of the 1953 Academy Award-winning movie) and 'I Dreamed Of A Hillbilly Heaven.' He also co-hosted the *Town Hall Party* radio and TV series from 1953 through 1960.

In 1965 Tex moved to Nashville, joining the Grand Ole Opry and hosting the popular radio WSM Radio show *Opry Star Spotlight*. He had been elected to the Country Music Hall of Fame in 1964 and also had a seat on the Country Music Association's Board of Directors.

On January 2, 1974, while visiting his guitar player who had been jailed in Nashville for failing to pay alimony, Ritter collapsed with a heart attack and died shortly after.

MARTY ROBBINS

Martin David Robinson was born in Glendale, Arizona on September 26, 1925.

When Marty was 12, his family moved to Phoenix. It wasn't until Marty's 3-year hitch in the Navy that he learned to play the guitar. Upon his discharge, he returned to Phoenix, digging ditches, driving a truck and working in the oil fields.

Working with a group called the K-Star Cowboys on KTYL Radio in Mesa, Arizona, Marty soon had his own show on Phoenix's KPHO radio during the late Forties, where guest star Jimmy Dickens "discovered" Marty and got him a record deal. (Marty also hosted a Phoenix television show, *Western Caravan* in 1951 and, years later, the nationally-syndicated *Marty Robbins Spotlight*.)

Marty began recording in 1952, beginning his 21-year-long stint with Columbia Records with a Number 1 single, 'I'll Go On Alone.' In 1953 Robbins (the singer shortened his surname and altered the spelling) joined the Grand Ole Opry. (Marty was fired by the Opry on March 1, 1958 following an argument with WSM Radio station manager Robert Cooper, but was rehired 5 days later after an exchange of apologies.)

By 1956, Robbins had established himself as a crossover artist with another Number 1 hit, 'Singing the Blues,' continuing the pattern of Number 1 crossover hits with 'A White Sport Coat (And A Pink Carnation)' and 'The Story Of My Life' (both 1957), 'Just Married' (1958), 'El Paso' (1959), 'Don't Worry' (1961), 'Devil Woman' and 'Ruby Ann' (1962).

In 1983, Marty, nicknamed "Ol' Golden Throat", and his fellow Opry artist Jeanne Pruett charted with their duet version of Pruett's composition 'Love Me'. Each artist also had a solo hit recording of the song.

Robbins MCed the closing portion of the Grand Ole Opry, not only because he was so popular that no one wanted to follow him, but also because he had a tradition of driving WSM MCs crazy by ignoring their tight time cues and offering to entertain the audience through to the daylight hours.

A two-time Grammy Award-winner, Robbins was inducted into the Country Music Hall of Fame just months before his death from heart disease on December 8, 1982.

JIMMIE RODGERS

James Charles Rodgers was born on September 8, 1897 in Meridian, Mississippi.

The son of Aaron Rodgers, a railroad section foreman, Jimmie spent his youth hanging around railroad yards. At 14 he became a railroadman, first serving as a water-boy and later as his father's assistant foreman.

Jimmie learned the trainmen's ballads, picking up his trademark yodel, a wail sounding like the whistle of an oncoming train, and the melancholy vocal style of drawing out the lyrics to his songs that became his signature. He also learned to play a variety of stringed instruments, including ukelele, guitar, banjo and mandolin.

As a railroad worker, Jimmie was exempted from military service in the First World War, but the loss of a good friend in the war inspired him to write the song that would become his first hit, 'Soldier's Sweetheart.'

Married in 1924 to the former Carrie Cecil Williamson, Jimmie was stricken that fall with tuberculosis. After three months in hospital, he was told that his days of working on the railroad were over and ordered to pursue less strenuous work.

Rodgers' attention turned to music and he started working with medicine shows around Tennessee and Kentucky, seeing a slight improvement in his health about the time he bought a road show of his own. But Jimmie's undying love of the railroad took him, his wife and daughter, Carrie Anita, to Florida where Rodgers became a brakeman on the Florida East Coast Railroad for nearly a year. Florida's moist coastal air, coupled with job strain which undermined his health, convinced him to move first to Tucson, Arizona, then to San Antonio and then to Galveston, Texas, all the while insisting that his family return to Meridian where he would eventually join them.

By January 1927, his health slightly improved, Jimmie found a job as a "special officer" on Asheville, North Carolina's police force and moved his family to Asheville. By May of 1927, Jimmie and three other Asheville country musicians were appearing on WWNC Radio as "the Jimmie Rodgers Entertainers." Rodgers, billing himself as "the Singing Brakeman," then took his hillbilly string quartet on the road playing one-nighters.

Jimmie next journeyed to Bristol, Tennessee where he met Victor Talking Machine Company talent scout Ralph Peer, who was holding auditions in Bristol. On August 4, 1927 Jimmie cut two sides of his first record, 'Sleep, Baby, Sleep,' a traditional yodeling lullaby, and 'Soldier's Sweetheart,' receiving a short-term contract from Peer on the spot.

Weeks later, in Camden, New Jersey, Rodgers recorded four more sides, including 'T For Texas' (also known as 'Blue Yodel No. 1'). Asked to cut 12 additional sides (which he did in spurts, fighting off a chronic tuberculin cough with swallows of whiskey), Jimmie came to the attention of Ray McCreath, an announcer for WTFF Radio in Washington, DC, and later Rodgers' show manager. It was McCreath who dubbed Jimmie

Jimmie Rodgers was one of country music's earliest stars and Hall of Fame inductees.

"America's Blue Yodeler." With record royalties by now an astounding $2,000 a month, England, Canada, and South America were all calling for Rodgers, but Jimmie's frailty made it impossible for him to travel.

By 1931 he had built a $50,000 home ("Blue Yodeler's Paradise") and worked with such famous folks as Will Rogers, Gene Austin, Louis Armstrong and the Carter Family.

On May 26, 1933, while in New York City to record and to negotiate a new contract with Ralph Peer, Jimmie died of tubercular pneumonia. He was inducted into the Country Music Hall of Fame in 1961.

JOHNNY RODRIGUEZ

Though Juan Raul Davis Rodriguez was born in Sabinal, Texas (on December 10, 1951) English was his second language. A Chicano, Rodriguez first learned to speak Spanish.

At the age of 7, Johnny was playing guitar and during his high school days he played in a rock band. Using the stage name Johnny Rogers, Rodriguez entertained at

Texas' Alamo Village Park (the widely-circulated story about Johnny being brought to Alamo Village after taking the rap for stealing and barbecuing a goat was created for publicity purposes) where he was discovered by Bobby Bare and Tom T. Hall.

Johnny moved to Nashville in 1971 with only a guitar and $14 in his pocket. He called Hall's office in search of a job, only to find Hall, whose guitarist, Pete Blue, had given notice, was looking for him! Johnny fronted the Hall's Storytellers until he began to steal the show, thanks to Tom's helping him to get a record deal, and to Hall's brother, Hillman, writing him a signature song first release, the 1972 'Pass Me By.'

Johnny, who has had half a dozen Number 1 solo hits, including 'You Always Come Back (To Hurting Me),' 'Ridin' My Thumb To Mexico,' and 'Love Put A Song In My Heart,' has had one hit duet record, a 1979 release, 'I Hate The Way I Love It,' with Charley McClain.

KENNY ROGERS

Kenneth Ray Rogers was born in Houston, Texas on August 21, 1938. During the mid

Kenny Rogers has faded in America in recent years, but he is still a favorite in Europe.

Fifties two friends who sang with Rogers in the church choir banded together and, calling themselves the Scholars, landed a recording contract. The Scholars had some regional success, but soon disbanded.

At 19, Rogers had a regional rock hit, 'That Crazy Feeling,' that garnered him a guest appearance on American Bandstand. But Kenny's greatest success during the early years came when he worked with groups, first as a bassist for a jazz group called the Bobby Doyle Trio, then moving on to become a "third generation" member of the New Christy Minstrels, three of whom joined Kenny to become the late Sixties rock group the First Edition.

Some of Kenny's hits with the First Edition also charted country (for example, 'Ruby, Don't Take Your Love To Town' and 'Ruben James'), but by 1973, with his group days behind him, Rogers embarked on a solo country career. In 1977 Kenny had his first Number 1 country record, 'Lucille,' a crossover hit that went gold, as did his subsequent releases, 'She Believes in Me,' 'Coward of the County' and 'Lady.'

Best known for his signature song, 'The Gambler,' Rogers has had a slew of duet partners including Dottie West, Dolly Parton, Ronnie Milsap, Sheena Easton and Kim Carnes. A five-time CMA award winner, Kenny Rogers has also won three Grammys and has a dozen platinum albums to his credit.

ROY ROGERS

Leonard Franklin Slye was born in Cincinnati, Ohio on November 5, 1911.

Moving to California in 1930, Slye played in bands such as the Hollywood Hillbillies, the Rocky Mountaineers and Jack and his Texas Outlaws, before forming his own group, the International Cowboys.

Len formed the Pioneer Trio, with Tim Spencer and Bob Nolan, the nucleus for the sextet that became the Sons of The Pioneers in 1933 when brothers Hugh and Karl Farr and Lloyd Perryman joined up.

Taking the stage names Dick Weston and then Roy Rogers, Slye went solo in 1937 and in 1938 took his first starring film role as a singing cowboy in *Under Western Stars.* Roy (who married Frances Octavia "Dale Evans" Smith in 1947) starred in 91 feature films before he and Dale moved on to television where they made 101 half-hour westerns.

Rogers, who began his recording career in 1946, had such hits as 'A Little White Cross On the Hill' and 'Lovenworth,' as well as several hits with other artists such as K. T. Oslin, the Oak Ridge Boys, Lorrie Morgan, and Restless Heart, who appeared on the 1991 *Roy Rogers Tribute* LP.

Roy Rogers is the only member to be twice inducted into the Country Music Hall of Fame, first, in 1980, with the other Original Sons Of The Pioneers, and then again in 1988.

SAWYER BROWN

Sawyer Brown, a quintet named after Nashville's Sawyer Brown Road, was formed in Music City during the late Seventies by lead singer Mark Miller and former vocalist and lead guitarist Bobby Randall.

Originally named Savanna, the group (including Gregg "Hobie" Hubbard on keyboards, Jim Scholten on bass, and drummer Joe Smyth) competed on the US TV series *Star Search* in 1984, winning $100,000 and landing a record contract. The group's second release, the 1985 'Step That Step,' became a Number 1 record. Other hits followed, including 'Betty's Bein' Bad' and 'The Walk.' Along the way, Sawyer Brown had a hit record singing along with the Oak Ridge Boys' Joe Bonsall on 'Out Goin' Cattin' in 1986.

Duncan Cameron replaced Bobby Randall in 1991.

JEAN SHEPARD

One of 11 children, Jean Shepard was born in Pauls Valley, Oklahoma on November 21, 1933.

Jean formed one of country music's earliest all-female bands, the Melody Ranch Girls, in the late Forties. The first female country singer to be with the Grand Ole Opry over 35 years, Shepard claims several other firsts: the first woman in country music to sell one million records, the first country female vocalist to overdub her voice and the first to make a color television commercial.

Discovered by Hank Thompson who saw her perform when he and the Melody Ranch Girls appeared on the same show, Jean credits Hank with being personally responsible for her receiving her first recording contract with a major label (Jean made her first recording when she was 15).

Shepard became a major country star following the release of her first Number 1 record in 1953, 'A Dear John Letter.' A crossover hit, Ferlin Husky contributed the recitation portion of the song, but he was not credited on the earliest records pressed. (Copies of 'A Dear John Letter' which don't credit Husky are now collectors' items.) 'A Dear John Letter' was so popular that, three months after its release, Jean and Ferlin released a sequel, 'Forgive Me John,' which, like its predecessor, was a crossover hit.

Jean joined the Grand Ole Opry on her 22nd birthday in 1955 and in the same year became a national TV star, featuring on Red Foley's "Ozark Jubilee". More hits followed, including 'A Satisfied Mind,' (released within months of Porter Wagoner's hit), 'Beautiful Lies,' 'Slippin' Away' and 'I'll Take The Dog,' the latter a duet recorded with fellow Grand Ole Opry star Ray Pillow in 1966.

Jean was eight months pregnant with her second child when her husband, Opry star Hawkshaw Hawkins, was killed in the 1963 plane crash that also claimed the lives of Patsy Cline and Cowboy Copas.

RICKY SKAGGS

Ricky Skaggs was born in Cordell, Kentucky on July 18, 1954.

At the age of 5, he attended a Bill Monroe concert where he was brought on stage. The toddler received a standing ovation for his version of 'Ruby' which he sang while playing Monroe's mandolin. By his teens Ricky was also playing acoustic guitar, fiddle and banjo. During his teen years and early twenties, Skaggs played in several bluegrass bands, releasing his first solo album, *That's It!*, in 1975.

Ricky's neo-traditionalist style of bluegrass brought the music new fans and in 1981 Skaggs had his first hits, 'Don't Get Above Your Raisin'' and 'You May See Me Walkin''. Ricky's many Number 1 hits include 'I Don't Care,' 'Heartbroke,' and the first bluegrass record by a solo artist ever to top the *Billboard* country chart, 'Uncle Pen.'

The Country Music Association's 1985 Entertainer of the Year and the CMA's 1982 Male Vocalist of the Year, Skaggs has also won three Grammy Awards. Together, Ricky and his wife Sharon White won the CMA's 1987 Vocal Duo of the Year honors for their Top 10 duet, 'Love Can't Ever Get Better Than This.'

Skaggs produces his own records as well as those of other artists (for example, Dolly Parton and the Whites), his perfectionist style leading to his nickname "Picky Ricky."

MARGO SMITH

Betty Lou Miller was born in Mutual, Ohio on April 9, 1939.

The only child of divorced parents, Betty Lou was raised by an aunt and uncle who later adopted her. While in high school, she sang with the Apple Sisters vocal group.

Betty Lou was an education major in college and she recorded her first album in Chicago while she was still teaching. The album received favorable reviews locally, so Betty Lou took it to Nashville. Betty Lou Smith (she had married for the first time) found Nashville to be equally receptive to her work as a singer and songwriter so, changing her name to Margo, she moved to Music City in 1973.

In 1975 she had her first Top 10 hit, 'There I've Said It.' During the next 2 years Smith had several hits and "The Tennessee Yodeler," as she came to be known, was honored in 1977 by being asked to appear on the *New Faces Show* presented at the annual Country Radio Broadcasters convention in Nashville.

Margo had Number 1 records with her covers of pop hits such as 'Don't Break The Heart That Loves You' (released by Connie Francis in 1962) and 'It Only Hurts For A Little While' (a 1956 hit for the Ames Brothers).

Smith's duet partners included Norro Wilson and Tom Grant, but her most successful duets were with Rex Allen, Jr: 'Cup of Tea,' (1980) and 'While The Feeling's Good' (1981), the latter a remake of a Mike Lunsford hit.

HANK SNOW

Clarence Eugene Snow was born in Brooklyn, Queens Country, Nova Scotia, Canada on May 9, 1914.

An abused child, at 12 Snow was working as a cabin boy in the Merchant Marine. When he returned from one of his trips, Hank's mother gave the boy a cheap mail order guitar. Hank, who idolized Jimmie Rodgers so much he would later name his son Jimmie Rodgers Snow, practiced his guitar, patterning himself after his childhood hero, and, with the encouragement of friends, began to work at clubs and at Halifax's CHNS Radio.

A featured act on *The Canadian Farm Hour*, Hank formed his Rainbow Ranch Boys band, calling himself "The Singing Ranger." In 1936 Snow signed his first recording contract with RCA Victor, Canada, but he moved to the United States in the mid Forties, working on the WWVA *Wheeling Jamboree*. By the late Forties

Hank had a lifetime contract with RCA Records, but hasn't recorded for the label in years.

Hank had worked in Hollywood with his performing horse Shawnee, and had moved on to KRLD in Dallas.

'I'm Movin' On,' Hank's 1950 signature song, was the first of three successive Number 1 hits he recorded (the others being 'The Golden Rocket' and 'Rhumba Boogie') and the song that brought Snow an invitation to join the Grand Ole Opry that year. Snow recorded a total of 85 chart singles from over 80 albums between 1949 and 1980, including his gold record 'I Don't Hurt Anymore.' Hank's duet partners have included Chet Atkins and Kelly Foxton.

A United States citizen, Snow presides over the Hank Snow Child Abuse Foundation. Hank was inducted into the Country Music Hall of Fame in 1979.

THE STATLER BROTHERS

The Staunton, Virginia-based quartet of brothers Harold and Don Reid and their childhood friends, Lew DeWitt and Phil Balsley, first called themselves the Kingsmen when they began singing in 1955. They subsequently renamed themselves the Statler Brothers (a name reflecting the group's whimsical nature in that none are named Statler and only two are brothers) when, searching for just that right name in a hotel room one night, they happened to glance at the brand name of a box of tissues.

During the early Sixties, the Statler Brothers auditioned for Johnny Cash, signing with Cash's label, Columbia Records, and touring with Cash for nearly 8 years as his opening act. Their 1965 single, 'Flowers On The Wall' (written by the group's tenor singer, DeWitt) was a pop and country smash. Their follow-up hits, such as 'Ruthless,' the punningly-titled 'You Can't Have Your Kate and Edith, Too,' 'Do You Remember These' and 'The Class Of '57' established the Statlers as masters of comic and nostalgic material.

Harold (the group's bass singer and chief comic) and Don (the lead singer and Statlers' spokesman) write most of the Statler Brothers' material, while baritone Phil Balsley is known as the quiet Statler. The Statlers once recorded under the names of their comic *alter egos*, Lester "Roadhog" Moran and the Cadillac Cowboys. During the early Eighties, the late Lew DeWitt left the group and was replaced by Jimmy Fortune.

Three-time Grammy winners, the Statler Brothers have received CMA Vocal Group of the Year honors nine times (including 6 consecutive years), and so consistently dominated the erstwhile Music City News Awards that the veracity of the publication's voting procedure was called into question. The result? Each of the Statlers' wins was legitimate.

Today, the Statler Brothers (or the Statlers, as they are interchangeably billed) host their own weekly series on The Nashville Network.

Featuring regulars Rex Allen, Jr and Janie Frickie, the *Statler Brothers Show* is not only the most popular show on TNN, it is the highest-rated musical variety show on any of the American networks.

RAY STEVENS

Harry Ray Ragsdale was born in Clarksdale, Georgia on January 24, 1939.

A disk jockey at 15, by 1957 Ray had a recording contract, but his first major hit did not come until 1961. Titled 'Jeremiah Peabody's Polyunsaturated Quick Dissolving Fast Action Pleasant Tasting Green And Purple Pills,' the song typed Stevens as a novelty song singer. With songs like 'Ahab the Arab,' 'Harry The Hairy Ape,' and 'Gitarzan,' Ray, the number-one novelty song artist, has kept audiences laughing for the past 35 years.

Numerous appearances on Andy Williams' long-running TV series (the same musical variety show that launched the Osmond Brothers' career) during the Sixties resulted in Ray's having his own network series during the summer of 1970.

While Stevens has had more success recording novelty songs, he has had some "serious" hits, such as 'Mr Businessman' (1968), and his first major pop and country hit, the 1970 gold record 'Everything Is Beautiful.'

GARY STEWART

Gary Stewart was born in Payne Gap, Kentucky on May 28, 1944. Raised in Fort Pierce, Florida, Gary began recording in 1964 on the Cory label. During the mid Sixties, he played in a rock band called the Amps. During the Seventies, he was hired by Charley Pride as his pianist. Signed to RCA in the early Seventies, Stewart charted country with his cover of the Bob Seger System's 1968 rock hit, 'Ramblin' Man.'

His 1974 Top 10 releases, 'Drinkin' Thing' and 'Out of Hand,' typed him as a singer of drinkin' and honky-tonkin' songs, an image reinforced by his next release and his only Number 1, the 1975 'She's Acting Single (I'm Drinkin' Doubles).'

Gary released duets with Dean Dillon in 1982 and 1983 and is still recording in the Nineties, but the songs he cut during the Seventies as a solo artist remain his most popular work.

DOUG STONE

Doug, who claims both the Georgia cities of Newnan (home of Alan Jackson) and Marietta (home of Travis Tritt) as his hometowns, was born June 19, 1956.

Doug Brooks, as he was known back then, first performed at the age of 7 at a Loretta Lynn show. At 15, he was writing songs and recording. At 16, he had built his own studio.

Trained as a diesel mechanic, Doug has performed music since he was 19, though he didn't land a recording contract until he turned 32. Success came quickly and Doug took on the stage surname Stone so as not to be confused with Garth Brooks. His first Epic single, the 1990 Grammy-nominated 'I'd Be Better Off In A Pine Box,' was the first of five Top 5 hits from Stone's first self-titled, platinum-selling album.

By the time his second album, *I Thought It Was You*, was released, hits like the title song and 'These Lips Don't Know How To Say Goodbye' were establishing Stone as country music's romantic balladeer.

Doug recorded his third album, *From The Heart* (a gold album featuring 'Warning Labels,' 'Too Busy Being In Love' and 'Made For Lovin' You') prior to his undergoing quadruple heart bypass surgery which resulted in a change of lifestyle for the self-admitted "greaseaholic."

Doug has received several award nominations from the Country Music Association and the Academy of Country Music.

GEORGE STRAIT

Born in Pearsall, Texas on May 18, 1952, George Harvey Strait taught himself guitar by studying a Hank Williams songbook while serving in Hawaii during the early Seventies. There George's base commander persuaded Strait to lead a country band, which George did before returning home to enroll in Southwestern Texas State University where he pursued a degree in agriculture.

Cattle ranching paid Strait's bills when he returned stateside. He signed with a small label in the late Seventies,

George Strait's clean-cut good looks have endeared him to female fans.

but Strait and his Ace In The Hole band hit their stride when George signed with MCA Records and released 'Unwound,' his first Top 10 record, in 1981.

With a string of Number 1 hits like 'The Chair,' 'I Cross My Heart,' and 'The Heartland,' George's clean-cut good looks have made a movie star of the Country Music Association's Entertainer of the Year for 1989 and 1990. His films include *The Soldier* and *Pure Country*.

A movie soundtrack for *Pure Country* (George's seventeenth MCA Records album), featuring the title cut, 'The King of Broken Hearts', and a cover of ErnestTubb's 1961 hit 'Thoughts Of A Fool,' has gone double platinum.

All of George's MCA catalogue up to February 1993 has gone either gold or platinum.

MARTY STUART

John Marty Stuart was born in Philadelphia, Mississippi on September 30, 1958.

Inducted into the Grand Ole Opry on November 28, 1992, Stuart is no stranger to the Opry stage, having begun his country music career at the age of 13 as a fully-fledged member of Lester Flatt's Nashville Grass bluegrass band.

After Flatt's death in 1979, Stuart joined Johnny Cash's band, becoming, for a time, Johnny's son-in-law by marrying Cash's daughter, Cindy. Marty left Johnny's band in 1985 to embark on a solo career, in which, ironically, his musicianship has been overshadowed by his fame as a vocalist.

Stuart's first release for Columbia Records, 'Arlene,' was a Top 20 hit. But Marty's next records didn't do so well. Suddenly, Stuart found himself without a label deal, just as his marriage was breaking up. But he bounced back with a new MCA Records contract, and hits such as 'Hillbilly Rock,' 'Tempted,' 'That's Country' and 'High On A Mountaintop' quickly re-established him. Stuart also joined his friend and fellow Opry star Travis Tritt on the famed No Hats Tour as a result of the singers' success with the duet 'The Whiskey Ain't Workin' Any More'.

Marty's This One's Gonna Hurt You LP featuring the title song went gold in 1993.

NAT STUCKEY

Nathan Wright Stuckey II was born in Cass, Texas on December 17, 1933, but grew up in Atlanta, Texas.

Nat, an announcer for Atlanta's KALT Radio, moved on to Shreveport, Louisiana's KWKH Radio where he wrote his first Number 1 hit, 'Waitin' In Your Welfare Line,' later a Number 1 record for Buck Owens in 1966. (Nat also wrote Jim Ed Brown's 1967 hit, 'Pop A Top.')

Stuckey had his own band, the Cornhuskers, from 1958 through 1959 and performed on the Louisiana Hayride from 1962 through 1966. In the latter year he had his first hit with his signature song, 'Sweet Thang,' a song he wrote as a duet but recorded himself when there were no takers. (Ironically, Ernest Tubb and Loretta Lynn recorded 'Sweet Thang' in 1967.)

In 1967, Stuckey formed the Sweet Thangs band, touring on the strength of his first and subsequent hits such as 'Plastic Saddle,' 'Sweet Thang and Cisco,' 'Take Time To Love Her' and 'I Used It All On You.' Nat and Grand Ole Opry star Connie Smith recorded two hit duets: in 1969 'Young Love' (a cover of simultaneously-released Fifties hits by Sonny James and Tab Hunter), and in 1970 'If God Is Dead (Who's That Living In My Soul).'

Stuckey, whose deep, resonant voice lent itself to voice-overs and jingles when he wasn't recording, died of lung cancer on August 24, 1988.

HANK THOMPSON

Known for his ever-present smile, his blend of Western swing and honky-tonk music, and his mastery of musical technology, Henry William Thompson was born in Waco, Texas on September 3, 1925.

During his teens, Hank performed original compositions on WACO Radio's noontime program (the only musical instruction he ever had was 12 guitar lessons), where Thompson was billed as "Hank, the Hired Hand." Hank served in the US Navy during the Second World War and studied at Southern Methodist University, the University of Texas and at Princeton. In August 1946 Thompson and his group, the Brazos Valley Boys, did a session in Dallas, Texas for Globe Records, leading to Hank's receiving a contract from Capitol Records the following year.

Hank's composition 'Humpty Dumpty Heart' became his first hit recording for Capitol in 1948, peaking at Number 2. His signature song, 'The Wild Side Of Life,' released in 1952, was a Number 1 crossover hit and a gold record for Hank. Thompson had nearly 80 chart releases for Capitol between 1948 and 1983, including 'Oklahoma Hills' and the Number 1 hits 'Rub-A-Dub-Dub' and 'Wake Up, Irene.' Hank was inducted into the Country Music Hall of Fame in 1989.

Hank Thompson brings a special blend of western swing and the honky-tonk sound to country music.

MEL TILLIS

Lonnie Melvin Tillis was born in Tampa, Florida on August 8, 1932.

Raised in Pahokee, Florida, where he developed a stutter after contracting malaria at the age of 3, Mel was a high school drummer and football player. He served in the Air Force and worked on the railroads before moving to Nashville in 1957, where he has made his mark as a songwriter (more than 500 of his songs have been recorded), singer, actor and comedian.

Mel began recording for Columbia Records in 1958, but it wasn't until 1972 that he had his first

Number 1 record, a cover of Webb Pierce's 1959 hit, 'I Ain't Never' (co-written by Pierce and Tillis). Mel's other Number 1 hits have included 'Good Woman Blues,' 'Heart Healer,' 'I Believe In You,' 'Coca Cola Cowboy' and 'Southern Rains.'

Tillis' duet partners have included Sherry Bryce, Glen Campbell, Bill Phillips, Webb Pierce and Nancy Sinatra. Featured on *The Porter Wagoner Show*, Tillis gained fame as a semi-regular on *The Glen Campbell Goodtime Hour* and later hosted his own syndicated TV show.

The Country Music Association's 1976 Entertainer of the Year, Tillis held ownership in Sawgrass, Cedarwood and other Nashville music publishing companies until 1987. Having published his autobiography, *Stutterin' Boy*, in 1984, he now entertains tourists at the Mel Tillis Theatre in Branson, Missouri.

PAM TILLIS

Pamela Yvonne Tillis was born in Plant City, Florida on July 24, 1957, the oldest of Mel and Doris Tillis's five children. Raised in Nashville, Pam's first performance was at the age of 8 when she sang a duet with Mel on the Grand Ole Opry.

Tillis was a rock 'n' rolling singer, songwriter, guitarist and pianist before deciding to follow in the footsteps of her singer/songwriter father. A staff writer for *Tree International* since 1990, Tillis has written songs recorded by Chaka Kahn, Juice Newton, Highway 101, Ricky Van Shelton, Conway Twitty and the Forester Sisters.

Though Pam first made the country charts back in 1984, it wasn't till 1991 that she had her first Number 1 single, 'Don't Tell Me What To Do,' from her gold album, *Put Yourself In My Place*. Other hits quickly followed, including 'One Of Those Things,' 'Put Yourself In My Place,' 'Maybe It Was Memphis,' 'Melancholy Child' (the latter is autobiographical) and, from Pam's *Homeward Looking Angel* LP, 'Shake The Sugar Tree,' 'Let That Pony Ride' and 'Cleopatra, Queen Of Denial.'

A film buff, Tillis lists her other hobbies as reading and collecting antiques.

AARON TIPPIN

Aaron Tippin (who pronounces his name A-run) was born in Florida on July 3, 1958, but reared in Traveler's Rest, South Carolina.

A pilot's son, Aaron received his own pilot's license at the age of 15, soloed at 16, and at 19 was a commercially licensed pilot. While studying to obtain a transport rating so that he could fly big jets, Aaron began to moonlight as a musician in the tri-state area of South Carolina, North Carolina and Georgia, playing in a bluegrass group called the Dixie Ridge Runners and then fronting Tip And The Darby Hill Band.

Aaron Tippin is country music's only tattooed bodybuilder.

In 1987 Aaron moved to Nashville and found success as a daily winner on The Nashville Network's erstwhile *You Can Be A Star* competition. Writing songs and pitching them along Nashville's Music Row by day, Tippin continued to support himself by working the night shift in a nearby Russellville aluminum rolling mill. He quickly distinguished himself by writing songs recorded by the gospel group the Kingsmen, and Charley Pride and Mark Collie (Tippin and Collie co-wrote Collie's smash, 'She Wants Something With A Ring To It').

Aaron's first hit record, 'You've Got To Stand For Something' (from the album of the same name) peaked at Number 5, followed by 'She Made A Memory Out Of Me,' which typifies Tippin's trademark hillbilly honky-tonk sound. Aaron's second album, *Read Between The Lines*, features the title cut and Aaron's Number 1 record, 'There Ain't Nothin' Wrong With The Radio,' and his hit 'I Wouldn't Have It Any Other Way.'

While at a North Carolina motorcycle enthusiasts' "swap meet" some years ago, Aaron acquired a tattoo of the South Carolina state flag. The tattoo is visible every time he bares his bulging right arm in another favorite pastime, bodybuilding.

MERLE TRAVIS

Merle Robert Travis was born in Rosewood, Kentucky on November 29, 1917.

Known for his unique finger-picking guitar style called "Travis-picking," Merle played in several bands during his twenties and appeared on Cincinnati's WLW Radio's *Boone County Jamboree*, Pasadena, California's KXLA Radio, and NBC Radio's *Plantation Party*. Travis, who played an important role in the development of the solid-body guitar, inspired Chet Atkins' guitar style. (Atkins' daughter, Merle, is named for Travis.)

Merle, who wrote or co-wrote songs such as 'Dark As A Dungeon,' 'Sixteen Tons' and 'Smoke, Smoke, Smoke (That Cigarette),' was a regular on TV shows such as *Hometown Jamboree*, *Merle Travis and Company*, *Town Hall Party*, and Johnny Cash's eponymous ABC TV series.

Travis' hits as a recording artist include the Number 1 songs 'Divorce Me C.O.D.' (1946) and 'So Round, So Firm, So Fully-Packed' (1947). Merle and Hank Thompson teamed their version of the instrumental, 'Wildwood Flower' in 1955 and had a Top 5 record. Travis married Thompson's ex-wife, Dorothy.

Merle Travis was inducted into the Country Music Hall of Fame in 1977 and died in Tahlequah, Oklahoma on October 20, 1983.

RANDY TRAVIS

Randy Bruce Traywick was born near Marshville, North Carolina on May 4, 1959.

Randy was in a band at the age of 10 and was working local clubs by the time he was 14. Traywick worked at Country City, USA in Charlotte, North Carolina from 1976 through 1981, recording for the first time a single produced by country star Joe Stampley, in 1978.

Billed as Randy Ray, he moved to Nashville in 1981 where he worked as a singer, dishwasher and cook at the Nashville Palace until the mid Eighties when he signed with Warner Brothers Records. (He was passed over when he auditioned for The Nashville Network's *You Can Be A Star* competition.)

Once more his name was changed; this time to Randy Travis. Travis's first album, *Storms of Life*, went platinum within a year of its 1986 release and Randy became the first of a long line of young "country hunks" who repopularized traditional country music. His Number 1 records include 'On The Other Hand' (first released in 1985, this peaked at Number 65, hitting the top of the charts only when it was re-released in 1986 as the follow-up to his hit '1982'), 'Diggin' Up Bones,' 'Forever And Ever Amen' and 'I Told You So.'

A two-time Grammy and five-time Country Music Association award-winner, Randy joined the Grand Ole Opry in 1986.

TRAVIS TRITT

James Travis Tritt was born in Marietta, Georgia on February 9, 1963.

Tritt counts Merle Haggard, George Jones, Johnny Cash and Buck Owens among his earliest musical influences. Travis taught himself guitar at the age of 8, wrote his first song at 14 and by the time he was in his twenties was playing the bar circuit.

Travis' 1990 début album, *Country Club*, garnered him three Number 1 singles before earning platinum status. His second album, 1991's *It's All About To Change*, yielded four Number 1s and reached the double-platinum mark. Tritt's third album, *T-r-o-u-b-l-e*, features him singing his hits 'Lord Have Mercy On The Working Man' (with Tanya Tucker, Porter Wagoner, T. Graham Brown, Little Texas, Brooks and Dunn, and George Jones joining in on the chorus), 'Anymore,' 'Can I Trust You With My Heart' and the title song.

Travis, who joined the Grand Ole Opry in 1992, has strong opinions and is known for his candour.

The outspoken Travis Tritt brings forceful themes to his music.

ERNEST TUBB

Ernest Dale Tubb was born in Crisp, Texas on February 9, 1914.

A Texas radio stalwart during the mid Thirties (San Antonio's KQNO and Fort Worth's KGKO), Tubb first recorded in 1936 for Bluebird Records. In 1941, Ernest wrote and recorded his signature song, 'Walking The Floor Over You' By 1943, Tubb had moved to Nashville and joined the Grand Ole Opry. From 1944 through 1979 he had several Number 1 hits, including 'Soldier's Last Letter,' 'It's Been So Long, Darling' and 'Rainbow At Midnight.'

Nicknamed "the Texas Troubadour", or simply "ET", Tubb starred in such movies as *Fighting Buckaroo, Hollywood Barn Dance, Ridin' West* and *Jamboree*. Tubb had two hits in 1949, singing with the Andrews Sisters ('I'm Biting My Fingernails And Thinking of You' and 'Don't Rob Another Man's Castle'). He also had hits with the Wilburn Brothers, recording 'Mr Love' with Doyle and Teddy in 1957, and 'Hey, Mr Bluebird' in 1958.

Ernest recorded seven duets with Red Foley between 1949 and 1953 and four with Loretta Lynn between 1964 and 1969. 'Walking The Floor Over You,' covered by George Hamilton IV in 1965, became a hit again for Tubb in 1979 when Ernest was joined on the song by Merle Haggard, Chet Atkins and Charlie Daniels.

Tubb established the world-famous Ernest Tubb Record Shop in 1947, the same year he began a post-Opry live broadcast there that continues to this day under the aegis of his son, Opry star Justin Tubb (the mail order record shop now has four locations).

Ernest Tubb was elected to the Country Music Hall of Fame in 1965. He died of emphysema on September 6, 1984.

TANYA TUCKER

Born in Seminole, Texas on October 10, 1958, Tanya Denise Tucker was raised in Wilcox, Arizona, the daughter of Beau and Juanita Tucker and younger sister of La Costa (La Costa had a string of country hits between 1974 and 1982) and Don. By 1969

After being overlooked for many years, Tanya Tucker is finally coming into her own.

Tanya was appearing on local television in the Phoenix, Arizona area and at the age of 13 she had her first hit, her signature song 'Delta Dawn.' Many Number 1 hits followed such as 'What's Your Mama's Name,' 'If It Don't Come Easy,' and 'It's A Little Too Late (To Do The Right Thing Now).'

Nicknamed "the Texas Tornado," Tucker recorded chart singles with Glen Campbell during 1980 and 1981. In 1987 she, Paul Davis and Paul Overstreet recorded a Number 1 single, 'I Won't Take Less Than Your Love' and Tucker joined T. Graham Brown on another hit duet, 'Don't Go Out With Him,' in 1990. Tanya's *What Do I Do With Me* went platinum while her gold albums include a greatest hits package and *Can't Run From Yourself*.

Active in country music for over two decades, Tanya's first notable industry award came when the Country Music Association named Tanya its 1991 Female Vocalist of the Year.

CONWAY TWITTY

Named for the silent screen film star Harold Lloyd, Harold Lloyd Jenkins was born in Friars Point, Mississippi on September 1, 1933.

At the age of 4 Jenkins was learning guitar chords. At 10, when his family had moved to Helena, Arkansas,

Conway Twitty—"the High Priest of Country Music" and "the best friend a song ever had."

90

Harold formed his own band, the Phillips County Ramblers. At 12, he hosted his own local Saturday morning radio show.

Harold was offered a contract with baseball's Philadelphia Phillies when he was drafted into the Army. Stationed in Japan during the early Fifties, Jenkins played with a USO band, the Cimmarons, and by the time his hitch was up, had decided a music career would prevail over athletics.

Adopting a stage name which he took from the cities of Conway, Arkansas and Twitty, Texas, Conway Twitty became a rock music sensation with his first hit, 'It's Only Make Believe' in 1958. Later pop hits included 'Mona Lisa,' 'Danny Boy' and 'C'est Si Bon,' before his rock career ended in 1961.

Twitty then turned to his first love, country music. Though his records charted country in 1966 and 1967, it wasn't until 1968 that Twitty was taken seriously as a country artist. Following the release of the Top 5 hit, 'The Image of Me,' Twitty amassed Number 1 hits with 'Next In Line,' 'To See My Angel Cry,' 'Hello, Darlin'' and a total of more than 50 others, establishing Conway as the performer with more Number 1 singles than any other artist in any field of music. Frequent duet partners, Conway Twitty and Loretta Lynn had five consecutive Number 1 hits between 1971 and 1975. Conway began work on his Music Village (quickly dubbed and renamed Twitty City) tourist attraction in Hendersonville, Tennessee, just outside Nashville, in 1981. Having seen it become hugely popular with visitors from all over the world, he died at Springfield, Missouri on June 5, 1993.

PORTER WAGONER

Like fellow Grand Ole Opry star Jan Howard, Porter Wayne Wagoner (born August 12, 1927 in South Fork township) calls West Plains, Missouri, home (West Plains boasts Porter Wagoner Boulevard and Jan Howard Expressway).

As a teenager, Porter sang and played guitar on a 15-minute KWPM radio show sponsored by the grocery store that employed him as a meat cutter. He moved on to a weekly spot on Springfield, Missouri's KWTO in September 1951. RCA Records expressed interest in Wagoner the next year when he made his first recordings at KWTO.

In 1952 Porter began recording in Nashville but it wasn't until 1954, when he was featured on the *Ozark Jamboree*, that he had his first Top 10 record, 'Company's Comin'.' Wagoner's follow-up record, 'Satisfied Mind,' became his first Number 1 hit and his signature song.

Porter moved to Nashville in 1957 and joined the Grand Ole Opry. By 1961 he was the host of the television show bearing his name, the longest-running syndicated country music TV show in history. In 1962 Porter had his second and only other solo Number 1 *Billboard* country chart hit, 'Misery Loves Company.'

"Pretty Miss" Norma Jean and Opry star Jeannie Seely had been featured vocalists on Wagoner's TV show during much of the Sixties, but it was Dolly Parton, whose tenure lasted from 1967 through 1974, who is best-remembered as the program's female singer. Porter and Dolly recorded 21 charted duet singles and 15 duet albums released between 1967 and 1982, garnering them the Country Music Association's Vocal Group of the Year honors in 1968, and the CMA's Vocal Duo of the Year award in 1970 and 1971.

Known as "The Thin Man From West Plains," Wagoner, a three-time Grammy winner, is an alternating host of The Nashville Network's *Opry Backstage*.

BILLY WALKER

Billy Marvin Walker was born in Ralls, Texas on January 14, 1929.

Billy started singing at the age of 10 as a member of his family's gospel quartet. At 15, having won a talent contest, Walker received $3, a chocolate cake and the opportunity to host his own 15-minute radio show on KICA Radio in Clovis, New Mexico, 80 miles from Ralls.

After hitchhiking to and from Clovis for 3 years, Billy finished school, sang with a trio and worked with a band before joining Dallas' *Big D Jamboree*. He moved on to the *Louisiana Hayride* and the *Ozark Jubilee*, touring with

Hank Williams and fronting Hank Thompson's band along the way as the 6-ft. 3-in. performer variously billed as "the Traveling Texan," "the Masked Singer of Country Songs," and "the Tall Texan."

Billy, who had his first Top 10 single in 1954, joined the Opry in 1960, had a Number 1 record, 'Charlie's Shoes' (his signature song), in 1962, and during the Seventies hosted his own syndicated television show, *Country Carnival*.

Billy Walker recorded 'Ringgold Georgia' with Brenda Kaye Perry in 1977, and three duets with Barbara Fairchild, including a cover of the Everly Brothers' 1957 hit 'Bye Love' in 1980.

KITTY WELLS

See separate entry in the Legends section.

DOTTIE WEST

The oldest of ten children, Dorothy Marie Marsh was born on a McMinnville, Tennessee farm on October 11, 1932.

Dottie had her own radio show in Cookeville, Tennessee, singing as she earned her way through Tennessee Tech where she earned a music degree. Though Dottie first recorded in 1959, it wasn't until 1961, when

In her lifetime, Dottie West's music was overshadowed by her colorful reputation.

Jim Reeves heard her songs and recommended her to Chet Atkins, that she attracted major label interest. Chet signed Dottie to RCA Records.

Dottie first charted with a Top 30 hit in 1963. She won a Grammy in 1964 for 'Here Comes My Baby,' a Top 10 hit Dottie co-wrote with her then husband, steel guitarist Bill West (the song has since been recorded by over 100 other artists). Dottie's signature song 'Country Sunshine' peaked at Number 2 in 1972, becoming her highest charting record at the time (the song served as the basis for a Coca-Cola ad campaign). She had solo Number 1 hits in 1980 with 'A Lesson In Leavin'' and 'Are You Happy Baby.'

Dottie's duet partners include Jim Reeves in 1964 (West wrote Reeves' 1960 hit 'I Missed Me'), in 1966 her son, Dale West (who, aged 4, recorded 'Mommy, Can I Still Call Him Daddy' with Dottie), in 1970 Jimmy Dean, in 1969 and 1970 Don Gibson, with whom Dottie had four hits, and from 1978 to 1984 Kenny Rogers, with whom she had a total of six hits, including the Number 1 singles 'Every Time Two Fools Collide,' 'All I Ever Need Is You,' and 'What Are We Doin' In Love.' West's protégés include Larry Gatlin and Steve Wariner.

Dottie joined the Grand Ole Opry in 1964 and remained a member until her death on September 4, 1991 from injuries sustained in a car crash.

DON WILLIAMS

Donald Ray Williams was born in Floydada, Texas, on May 27, 1939.

Raised in Portland, near Corpus Christi, Don won an alarm clock as the first prize in a talent contest at the age of 3. He began playing guitar as a teenager and formed the pop/folk Pozo Seco Singers trio. They had the Top 10 pop hit 'Time' in 1964.

Don moved to Nashville in 1967 and began recording as a solo singer/songwriter when the trio disbanded in 1971. He had the first of his Number 1 hits in 1974 with 'I Wouldn't Want To Live If You Didn't Love Me.' Don has had more than 15 Number 1s, including 'It Must Be Love,' 'Say It Again' and 'Heartbeat In The Darkness.'

Don was the Country Music Association's Male Vocalist of the Year in 1978 and in 1981 he won the CMA's Album of the Year honors for I Believe In You.

Nicknamed "the Gentle Giant," the 6-ft. 1-in., 180-pound singer has five gold albums to his credit and was the first country artist to make a concept music video (1973's Come Early Morning).

Don's 1992 album Currents contains a cut, 'In The Family,' featuring Zimbabwe's Bhundu Boys. Williams' international popularity is further reflected in appearances he has made in England, France, Monaco, Belgium, Germany, Spain, Wales, Sweden, Scotland, Finland and Holland.

HANK WILLIAMS

See separate entry in the Legends section.

HANK WILLIAMS, JR

Technically, Hank Williams, Jr is not a junior! The son of Hiram King Williams, Hank Jr was christened Randall Hank Williams when he was born in Shreveport, Louisiana on May 26, 1949. Nicknamed "Bocephus" by his father, Hank Jr was raised in Nashville. He played his first show at the age of 8, acceding to pressure to fulfil a musical void left by his late father. Hank's first Top 5 single, 'Long Gone Lonesome Blues,' was the 15-year-old's imitation of his father's 1950 hit.

When he was 16, Hank wrote and recorded another Top 5 record, 'Standing In The Shadow,' a public admission that his father's artistry was something that could not be cloned. His first Number 1 record came in 1970: 'All For The Love Of Sunshine' from the movie *Kelly's Heroes*.

Following recuperation from a 1975 mountain climbing accident which nearly killed him, Hank re-evaluated his career and began making a more definite move away from his father's musical style. Alternately aligning himself with southern rockers and going in his own direction, Hank had a succession of Number 1 hits, three consecutive: 'Texas Woman,' 'Dixie On My Mind,' and 'All My Rowdy Friends (Have Settled Down).'

Twice voted the Country Music Association's Entertainer of the Year (in 1987 and 1988), Hank's list of duet partners includes Lois Johnson (with whom he recorded four duets between 1970 and 1972), Waylon Jennings (1983), Ray Charles (1985) and Doug Kershaw (1988).

TAMMY WYNETTE

Virginia Wynette Pugh was born near Tupelo, Mississippi on May 5, 1942.

Raised in Alabama, Wynette worked as a Birmingham beautician in the early Sixties, beginning her musical career on Birmingham's WBRC TV *Country Boy Eddy* show. She moved to Nashville in 1966 and, when she signed with Columbia Records, her producer and co-writer Billy Sherrill gave Wynette her new stage name: Tammy. Tammy's first releases were 'Apartment #9' and 'Your Good Girl's Gonna Go Bad.' In 1967 she had her first Number 1 record when she teamed with David Houston on 'My Elusive Dreams' (Tammy and David released 'It's All Over' in 1967). Wynette had four consecutive Number 1 records in 1968 and 1969: 'D-I-V-O-R-C-E,' 'Stand By Your Man' (her signature song), 'Singing My Song' and 'The Ways To Love A Man.' Tammy would have ten more Number 1 hits as a solo artist through 1988.

The list of those with whom Tammy has recorded reads like a veritable who's who of popular music. It includes Mark Gray (Wynette's 1985 duet with Gray, a cover of Dan Hill's 1978 pop hit 'Sometimes When We Touch,' peaked at Number 6), Michael Martin Murphey, Emmylou Harris, Ricky Skaggs, Vince Gill, the O'Kanes, Randy Travis, British rappers the KLF (the Wynette-KLF duet 'Justified And Ancient' was a Number 1 record in 18 countries), Elton John, Tom Petty, Bonnie Raitt, Dolly Parton and Loretta Lynn.

Tammy Wynette's musical persona has evolved with the times.

But the most popular pairing has been that of Tammy and her ex-husband, George Jones. George and Tammy recorded 10 duet albums and released 13 singles between 1971 and 1980 (three of their singles, 'We're Gonna Hold On,' 'Golden Ring' and a remake of the Francis Craig Orchestra's 1947 hit 'Near You' reached Number 1).

The First Lady of Country Music first toured England and Germany in 1966 and she's returned regularly to Europe ever since.

WYNONNA

She was named Christina Claire Ciminella when she was born in Ashland, Kentucky on May 30, 1964.

When she was 8, her parents, Michael and Diana Ciminella, divorced. Diana Ciminella reclaimed her maiden name of Judd and struggled to support the asthmatic Christina and her younger sister, Ashley, on a nurse's salary. The family spent some time in California, where Christina worked for the Fifth Dimension, and then settled in Franklin, Tennessee about 1980.

Having changed her name to Naomi during her time in California, Christina now changed it again, this time adopting the name of the Oklahoma town of Wynonna. By this time mother and daughter had formed a singing duo called

Formerly one half of mother-daughter duo the Judds, Wynonna is now a major solo artist.

the Judds and had appeared on *The Ralph Emery Show* on Nashville's WSM-TV, America's highest-rated early morning local TV show. By 1983 the Judds were signed to RCA Records. The duo had more than a dozen Number 1 records (eight of them consecutively) and sold six million records in the 7 years they spent together before poor health forced Wynonna's retirement.

'She Is His Only Need,' the début single from *Wynonna*, the singer's first solo album on MCA/Curb, was followed by 'No One Else On Earth,' 'Tell Me Why,' 'Only Love' and Wynonna's duet with Clint Black, 'A Bad Goodbye.'

TRISHA YEARWOOD

Patricia Lynn Yearwood was born in Monticello, Georgia, 60 miles south of Atlanta, on September 9, 1964.

Trisha left junior college to attend the University of Georgia, where she majored in business before transferring to Nashville's Belmont University where she received a music business degree.

While working as a secretary at MTM Records, she began making music business contacts and singing demos. One of these was with a fellow demo singer, Garth Brooks. When Brooks' solo career took off, he jump-started Trisha's career by choosing her to sing on his albums and to be his opening act.

Her 1991 self-titled début album, featuring Yearwood's Number 1 singles 'She's In Love With The Boy' and 'The Woman Before Me' followed by 'Like We Never Had A Broken Heart,' went platinum. Yearwood's second album, *Hearts In Armor* (containing 'Wrong Side Of Memphis' and 'Walkaway Joe') features Garth, Don Henley, Emmylou, Vince and the Maverick's Raul Malo.

Trisha made her silver screen début in the 1993 feature film, *The Thing Called Love*.

DWIGHT YOAKAM

Dwight David Yoakam was born in Pikesville, Kentucky on October 23, 1956.

Dwight played southern Ohio roadhouses before making an initial stop in Nashville—where he was told he was too country! In the early Eighties he moved to California, striking up a friendship with Buck Owens after showing up unannounced at Buck's office. In 1988, Dwight had his first Number 1 record, 'Streets Of Bakersfield,' a duet with Buck. He followed up with a solo Number 1 that year, 'I Sang Dixie.'

Dwight's *Guitars, Cadillacs, Etc.*, *Hillbilly Deluxe*, *Buenas Noches From A Lonely Room*, *Just Lookin' For A Hit* and *If There Was A Way* albums were either gold or platinum sellers.

In 1993 Yoakam released *This Time*, his first album in 3 years.

FARON YOUNG

Faron Young was born in Shreveport, Louisiana on February 25, 1932.

Young began his recording career in 1951 with Tillman Franks And His Rainbow Boys. Faron's mentor, Webb Pierce, got him on the *Louisiana Hayride* and the two toured together. Faron had his first of five Number 1 singles, 'Live Fast, Love Hard, Die Young,' in 1955. The others are 'Alone With You,' 'Country Girl' (his signature song), 'Hello Walls' and 'It's Four In The Morning.'

Founder and one-time publisher of the fan publication *Music City News* (once published in a building that now bears his name), Faron recorded three duets in 1964 with Margie Singleton.

Variously dubbed "the Young Sheriff," "the Singing Sheriff" and "the Sheriff" after a role he played in the 1956 movie *Hidden Guns*, Young was honored when American astronaut Charles "Pete" Conrad took tapes of his music aboard the Apollo 12 spacecraft.

When Dwight Yoakam first came to Nashville, record labels refused to sign him, calling his music "too country."

legends

ROY ACUFF

The King of Country Music

✪ ✪ ✪

Singer/Songwriter/Fiddler/Music Publisher/Actor
Born: September 15, 1903, Maynardsville, Tennessee
Died: November 23, 1992, Nashville, Tennessee

BORN IN A THREE-ROOM SHACK, THE THIRD OF NEIL AND IDA ACUFF'S FIVE CHILDREN, ROY CLAXTON ACUFF BEGAN PLAYING THE JEW'S HARP AND HIS FATHER'S FIDDLE WHILE A SMALL BOY. ACUFF'S UNUSUAL MIDDLE NAME (TO WHICH HE REFERS IN A LINE FROM HIS SIGNATURE SONG, 'WABASH CANNONBALL') COMES FROM A MAN ROY'S FATHER ADMIRED, AN EDUCATOR NAMED DR P. P. CLAXTON.

Roy's family moved to Fountain City, a suburb of Knoxville, in 1919. At Central High School Roy starred in the class plays and became the most celebrated athlete in the school's history, quite an accomplishment when one considers that he was very small for his age. Weighing just 130 pounds, Acuff was nicknamed "Rabbit". Roy lettered 12 times in 4 years. Returning to Central High a fifth year, he earned another letter—in baseball.

Despite his college-educated father's desire for Acuff to attend the University of Tennessee, Roy held a series of odd jobs while playing semi-professional baseball and basketball. Baseball was Acuff's first love. A pitcher, left-fielder, center-fielder and shortstop, he exhibited a versatility that brought him to the attention of some New York Yankee recruiters who invited Roy to the Yankees' Florida farm camp. While there, Roy went fishing, stayed out in the sun too long and caught a bad case of sunstroke. Confined to bed for 3 months, he warded off boredom by playing the fiddle. He also took up yo-yoing to pacify his urge to throw a baseball. By 1932 he had accepted an invitation to join a medicine show. He performed in drag for some of the sketches and played the fiddle.

After a summer with the medicine show, Roy decided music would be his career. Having formed a trio called the Three Rolling Stones, in 1933 he became part of a band called the Tennessee Crackerjacks who performed on Knoxville's WROL Radio before moving on to WROL's competitor, WNOX Radio, where Acuff performed on the station's famed *Midday Merry Go Round*.

Returning to WROL in 1935, Roy's band was renamed the Crazy Tennesseans. Acuff began his recording career in 1936. One of his sessions occurred on a particularly hot day, forcing Roy and his musicians to record in their underwear! Acuff

also married Mildred Douglas in 1936. Roy and Mildred, who had dated since 1929, became the parents of Roy Neill (who later recorded under the name Roy Acuff Jr) on July 25, 1943. The Acuffs also adopted a daughter, Thelma, who accompanied Roy's troupe as a tap dancer when Acuff toured military bases in Europe in 1949.

Roy's first recording session included his signature song, 'Great Speckle Bird' (later known as 'Great Speckled Bird'), and 'Wabash Cannonball.' Acuff joined the Grand Ole Opry in 1938 (he first appeared on the show in 1937), and changed his band's name to the Smoky Mountain Boys. Roy was nervous during his first Opry performance. His fiddling was not very good and he was disappointed in his overall performance as a result. However, he said later that the audience was sympathetic and that perhaps his performance of 'Great Speckle Bird' redeemed him in their eyes since he received four or five encores!

By 1940 Roy was a movie star, making his motion picture début in

Republic Pictures' *Grand Ole Opry*. This first of Acuff's eight films also featured appearances by Uncle Dave Macon, Roy's band, and the "Solemn Old Judge," the Opry master of ceremonies who first named the radio stage show the Grand Ole Opry, George D. Hay.

Roy's second movie, also for Republic, was 1942's *Hi Neighbor*, which also featured country music stars Lulu Belle and Scotty.

His third Republic picture, in which he played the part of a sheriff, was 1943's *Oh My Darling Clementine*. The movie also featured Irene Ryan, who went on to star as Granny Clampett in *The Beverly Hillbillies* television series.

Acuff's fourth film, a Columbia Pictures 1944 release called *Cowboy Canteen*, featured the Mills Brothers, Tex Ritter and Jimmy Wakely. Returning to Republic in 1944, Roy appeared in *Sing, Neighbor, Sing*, once again starring with Lulu Belle and Scotty, and Roy's own Smoky Mountain Boys.

In 1946, having briefly left the Opry because of conflicts in his schedule caused by movie-making and lucrative personal appearances, Roy starred in what he considered to be his best film, Republic's *Night Train to Memphis,* in which he sang the title song. Roy's seventh movie, *Smoky Mountain Melody,* a 1948 Columbia Pictures release, was followed by his final film, *Home in San Antone,* in 1949.

When Acuff wasn't making movies he was playing the Opry or touring. From 1939 to the mid Forties, Roy's musical family included five-string banjo player Rachel Veach. Since a woman traveling on the road with men was frowned upon during those days, Veach was billed as band member Bashful Brother Oswald's sister.

In 1942, Roy and pop music performer and songwriter Fred Rose pioneered music publishing in Nashville by forming Acuff-Rose Publishing, with writers of the stature of Pee Wee King and Redd Stewart. The latter co-wrote 'The Tennessee Waltz.' Hickory Records, a spin-off of the partnership, was formed in 1953, and the Acuff-Rose Artists Agency began booking country performers in 1965.

By 1944 Roy's recording career was in gear. He had three Top 10 hits that year: 'The Prodigal Son' and the double-sided hit, 'I'll Forgive You But I Can't Forget' and 'Write Me Sweetheart.' His popularity during the war years was so great that some music polls suggested it surpassed that of Frank Sinatra. (Roy sold a career total of over 30 million records.) Further evidence of the regard in which Acuff was held was reflected in a refrain the Japanese troops used to taunt American soldiers: "To hell with Roosevelt, to hell with Babe Ruth and to hell with Roy Acuff."

Back in Tennessee, Acuff was courted by both the Republicans and Democrats as gubernatorial candidate during 1943 and 1944. In 1946, speculation about Roy's political aspirations resurfaced but it wasn't until 1948 that he declared his candidacy for governor as a Republican. Roy lost the race, but the international country music community reclaimed him. Beginning in 1949,

Acuff made annual tours, appearing before servicemen stationed in Alaska, Germany, Korea, Japan, the Canal Zone, Austria, England, Iceland, Newfoundland, France, Italy, Bermuda, Spain, Guantanamo Bay, Morocco and the Dominican Republic.

In 1962 Roy was honoured by becoming the Country Music Hall of Fame's first living member.

During the Vietnam era, he entertained American troops, and in 1973 he performed for returning POWs at the Nixon White House. On March 16, 1974 it was Roy's turn to welcome President Richard Nixon to the Grand Ole Opry's début performance at its Opryland location. As Roy, the first performer to sing on the new Opry House stage, taught the president to yo-yo, Nixon (in the midst of the Watergate débâcle) told Roy

Roy Acuff, "King of Country Music" and pre-eminent star of the Opry.

that he was going to remain in Nashville and learn to yo-yo and that Acuff could go to Washington and be president!

While, in 1974, most of the older Opry stars opposed the move of the Opry from the Ryman Auditorium to its present location, citing the tradition of the old church building and the impersonal nature of a more modern structure, Roy surprised most by agreeing with the younger Opry stars that a larger facility with heating, air-conditioning, parking and dressing-rooms was a welcome change from the cramped quarters of the deteriorating Ryman. Acuff never requested his own assigned dressing room, but when the Opry moved to Opryland, dressing room Number 1 was given to the man baseball star Dizzy Dean once crowned "the King of the Hillbillies." (When the term "hillbilly" connoted derision rather than affection Roy was billed "the King of Country Music.") That honor was reciprocated by Acuff, whose dressing room door was always open to his colleagues. They responded by gathering frequently for informal jam sessions with the King. During Roy's lifetime no other performer used dressing-room Number 1, even during his infrequent absences.

Roy, the first country music performer to have a street on Nashville's Music Row (Roy Acuff Place) named after him, received the Grammy Lifetime Achievement Award in 1987 and, in 1991, just months before his death from congestive heart failure, he was presented with the Congressional Medal of Honor by President George Bush. Visitors to Nashville's Opryland theme park are given the opportunity to go through the Roy Acuff Museum and to pass by the home on the park grounds where Roy moved following his wife, Mildred's, death in 1981.

101

EDDY ARNOLD

The Tennessee Plowboy

✪ ✪ ✪

Singer/Songwriter/Movie Star/TV Host
Born: May 15, 1918, Henderson, Tennessee

RICHARD EDWARD ARNOLD WAS BORN ON A CHESTER COUNTY, TENNESSEE FARM ABOUT 140 MILES FROM HIS PRESENT-DAY HOME IN THE NASHVILLE SUBURB OF BRENTWOOD, TENNESSEE.

The youngest of five children, Eddy's first musical heroes were Gene Autry and Bing Crosby. Arnold learned to play his cousin's Sears Roebuck Silvertone guitar and, following his seventeenth birthday, left home for Jackson, Tennessee where he played guitar and sang on WTJS Radio. Arnold also worked area clubs before moving on to Memphis and St Louis and joining Pee Wee King's Golden West Cowboys in 1940.

Eddy married Sally Gayhart in 1941 and the two moved to Nashville with Pee Wee to work on WSM Radio. In 1943 Arnold left King and signed with RCA Records. In 1944, Eddy signed a management contract with Tom Parker (later known as Colonel Tom Parker, Elvis Presley's manager) and became one of the earliest singers to record in Nashville. (Arnold first recorded his signature song, 'Cattle Call,' at a WSM Radio studio, then in downtown Nashville. By 1993 he had recorded the song a total of four times.)

By 1945, the year Sally presented him with a daughter, Jo Ann, Eddy was having Top 10 records, and in 1947 he had three Numbers 1s: 'What Is Life

Without Love,' 'It's A Sin,' and Arnold's first gold record, 'I'll Hold You In My Heart (Til I Can Hold You In My Arms).' By 1947 Arnold was a radio veteran. Appearances on the Grand Ole Opry led to Eddy's being offered his own Ralston Purina-sponsored, 15-minute noontime Mutual Network radio show, *Checkerboard Square*.

During 1948 Arnold had three more gold records: 'Anytime,' 'Bouquet of Roses' and 'Just A Little Lovin' (Will Go A Long Way).' In 1949 he became a father again when his wife gave birth to a son, Richard Edward Arnold Jr. Arnold also became a film star at this time. He made two movies—*Feudin' Rhythm* and *Hoedown*—that were released in 1950. Arnold also made his television début in 1949: a guest spot on *The Milton Berle Show*.

Dubbed "the Tennessee Plowboy," Eddy became the first country performer to host his own network TV show, *The Eddy Arnold Show*, a musical variety series that was televised first on CBS, then on NBC and finally on ABC TV, from

July 14, 1952 through September 28, 1956. The program ran as a summer replacement series for Perry Como (on CBS) and Dinah Shore (on NBC) during its first two seasons. Only 15 minutes in length, Eddy's show was barely long enough to present more than two or three songs, but when the program moved to ABC in 1956 it was expanded to half an hour. The ABC series featured such artists as Chet Atkins and the Paul Mitchell Quartet, an instrumental group.

During 1967 Eddy was one of the rotating hosts of NBC TV's *Kraft Music Hall* and one of three stars—the others were comedians Don Rickles and Alan King—who appeared the most often during the series' run from 1967 through 1971.

Arnold was elected to the Country Music Hall of Fame in 1966 and named by the Country Music Association as its first Entertainer of the Year in 1967. In 1969 Eddy published his autobiography, *It's A Long Way From Chester County*, which details how he became one of country music's wealthiest entertainers as

a result of a series of investments, primarily in real estate. Eddy's business acumen has prompted many to joke that he virtually owns Brentwood, Tennessee! Today he serves on the Board of Directors of several banks and leading corporations.

The winner of the Academy of Country Music's Pioneer Award in 1984, Eddy won the Songwriters' Guild's President's Award in 1987. A recording artist for half a century, Arnold has sold over 85 million records, making him among the top-selling recording artists of all time. With the release of

his boxed set, *The Last Of The Love Song Singers* in 1993, he has one more achievement of which to be proud: he has had records in the charts in each of the last six decades!

Eddie Arnold, a country music star for no fewer than six decades.

GARTH BROOKS

Current King of Country

✦ ✦ ✦

Singer/Songwriter
Born: February 7, 1962, Tulsa, Oklahoma

TROYAL GARTH BROOKS IS THE YOUNGEST OF SIX CHILDREN OF TROYAL RAYMOND AND COLLEEN BROOKS. RAISED IN YUKON, 90 MILES FROM OKLAHOMA CITY, BROOKS CAME BY HIS MUSICAL ABILITY NATURALLY. AS COLLEEN CARROLL, HIS MOTHER RECORDED FOR CAPITOL RECORDS DURING THE FIFTIES AND PERFORMED WITH RED FOLEY ON THE *OZARK JUBILEE*.

But music took a back seat to sports during Garth's years at Yukon High School. Active in track and field, Garth also played baseball, football and basketball. A partial athletic scholarship, awarded for his javelin-throwing ability, took him to Oklahoma State University in Stillwater. While studying for the advertising degree that he received in 1984, he played in bands and worked as a bouncer. One night he threw out a girl called Sandy Mahl after a restroom altercation. In 1986 Sandy became Mrs Brooks.

This was following Garth's famous 23-hour "move" to Nashville in 1985, aborted when the cocky but naive would-be country sensation's dreams of stardom failed to materialize overnight. But a little maturity regarding the realization of his goals was all that stood in his way. In 1988 Garth signed with Capitol Records and released his first single, 'Much Too Young (To Feel This Damn Old),' from his self-titled album in July 1989.

That début single, which Garth co-wrote with Randy Taylor (Brooks has either written or co-written most of his hits) peaked at Number 10 in the *Billboard* chart. The next three singles from *Garth Brooks*—'If Tomorrow Never Comes,' 'Not Counting You' and 'The Dance'—were all Number 1 hits and the album has sold almost four million copies since its release in 1989.

Garth's second and third Capitol/Nashville albums, *No Fences* (1990) and *Ropin' The Wind* (1991), have each yielded four Number 1 singles and sold over nine and a half million copies. In addition, *Ropin' The Wind* made musical history by débuting on the *Billboard* Top 200 chart at Number 1.

Garth's Liberty albums include a Christmas album, *Beyond The Season*, which has sold two and a half million copies, and *The Chase*, which has sold over five million copies. *The Chase* features 'Somewhere In The Night' and the controversial single 'We Shall Be Free.'

In 1990 Garth became a Grand Ole Opry member and in 1991 won a Grammy (Best Country Performance, Male) for *Ropin' The Wind*. In 1991 also, Brooks won six Academy of Country Music Awards— one for every category in which he was nominated—including Entertainer of the Year. Garth is also the Country Music Association's reigning two-time Entertainer of the Year (1991 and 1992).

Noting that he has made more money than his children's children will ever be able to spend, Garth briefly contemplated retirement from country music during 1992, the year Sandy gave birth to their first child. He was afraid that he would not be able to balance the demands of fatherhood—his first priority—with an unrelenting tour schedule.

Some might view the characterization of Garth Brooks as a country music legend as being premature. But this much is clear: Garth's unsurpassed net worth and his great popularity have been statistically documented in record and ticket sales. His appeal transcends that of the country music audience and is international in scope.

Garth shows all the signs of staying power due to the loyalty of fans. He has repaid their loyalty time and again by, for example, holding down ticket prices, signing autographs for stretches longer than any artist appearing at Nashville's Fan Fair (until every request is fulfilled) and working for scale on consecutive Friday and Saturday nights at the Grand Ole Opry, even in the middle of summer when his concert schedule is at its busiest and most lucrative. Also, he has helped the careers of fellow artists such as Trisha Yearwood, Martina McBride and Stephanie Davis.

Garth Brooks: a new "King of Country" for the Nineties.

JOHNNY CASH

The Man in Black

✪ ✪ ✪

Singer/Songwriter/Author/Actor
Born: February 26, 1932, Kingsland, Arkansas

J. R. CASH (AS HE WAS CHRISTENED) IS ONE OF THE LATE RAY AND CARRIE CASH'S SEVEN CHILDREN. RAISED IN DYESS, ARKANSAS, CASH'S EARLIEST FAN WAS HIS MOTHER, WHO, REALIZING HER SON'S TALENT, SPENT MONEY THE IMPOVERISHED CASHES DIDN'T REALLY HAVE TO GIVE JOHN SINGING LESSONS. BUT THE VOCAL COACH, SO IMPRESSED WITH JOHN'S NATURAL ABILITY, SUGGESTED THAT SUCH LESSONS WEREN'T REALLY NECESSARY AND THE FORMAL TRAINING CEASED.

Cash first performed on the radio while he was still in high school. While serving in the Air Force, John (as his family and closest friends still call him) learned the guitar and wrote his first songs. Following his discharge in 1954, Cash and his wife, the former Vivian Liberto, moved to Memphis.

In the Bluff City John met Marshall Grant, a bass player, and Luther Perkins, an electric guitar player. Cash, Grant and Perkins began performing together—gratis—on Memphis Radio station KWEM. Each wore black shirts, black being a color which increasingly dominated John's stage wardrobe, earning him the nickname "The Man in Black."

Next, the trio auditioned for Sun Records' Sam Phillips, playing Cash's compositions, 'Hey, Porter,' and 'Cry, Cry, Cry.' Sun released the songs which became double-sided regional hits for Johnny Cash And The Tennessee Two, as the trio was now billed. In 1955, Cash's next Sun releases, 'So Doggone Lonesome' and 'Folsom Prison Blues,' each reached Number 4 on the country chart and, coupled with his earlier success, won him a spot on the *Louisiana Hayride*.

Cash's first national hit, his signature song 'I Walk the Line,' sold a million copies following its 1956 release and was Johnny's first Number 1 record and crossover hit. Cash joined the Grand Ole Opry in 1957 and by 1960, with the addition of a third musician (drummer W. S. "Fluke" Holland), Johnny Cash And The Tennessee Three was born. In 1966 Carl Perkins began touring with Johnny as a part of the Cash show, taking some of the pressure off Cash, who was succumbing to personal problems, including drug dependency and divorce. In 1968 Johnny married June Carter, with whom he shared his first Grammy Award for their duet recording of 'Jackson.'

The Country Music Association's 1969 Entertainer of the Year, Johnny hosted his highly popular self-titled ABC TV musical variety show from the Ryman Auditorium between 1969 and 1976. The program featured regulars Mother Maybelle and the Carter Family (Helen, June and Anita), the Statler Brothers, the Tennessee Three (Grant, Holland, and guitarist Bob Wooten, who joined Cash after the death of Luther Perkins) and made national stars of comedians Steve Martin and Jim Varney. The program also featured a weekly segment called "Ride This Train", bringing to life American history in story and song,

Johnny Cash: internationally, "the Man in Black" is probably the best known of all country music artists.

and it was particularly notable for a level of sophistication unmatched by either the syndicated country music television shows of its day or the network country shows of an earlier era. Viewers of the *Ozark Jubilee*, *The Jimmy Dean Show*, *Swingin' Country*, *The Eddy Arnold Show* and the like were not treated to what the Cash show offered: both an all-star country cast presented in a dignified setting, and the best of celebrated non-country talent, including Louis Armstrong, Arlo Guthrie, Linda Ronstadt, Bob Dylan, Pete Seeger and James Taylor. Additionally, most of these artists had some link with Johnny, whose eclectic musical tastes have led him to work with a great diversity of other performers. In 1993 Cash and Bono began writing songs together.

Cash's autobiography, *The Man in Black*, was published in 1975. In 1980, with nearly 140 chart singles to his name, he was elected to the Country Music Hall of Fame. In 1990 he received the National Association of Recording Arts and Sciences Legend Award.

PATSY CLINE

The Cline

✦ ✦ ✦

Singer
Born: September 8, 1932, Winchester, Virginia
Died: March 5, 1963, Camden, Tennessee

Opry Museum. In 1993 Hallway released a home video called *Remembering Patsy*. Produced by Charlie Dick, Cline's second husband, the video features the only known footage of Cline singing 'I Fall To Pieces', as well as a clip of country music star Michelle Wright reading Patsy's personal letters.

No one messed with "the Cline", as Patsy called herself.

BORN VIRGINIA PATTERSON HENSLEY, PATSY CLINE (CLINE WAS HER FIRST MARRIED NAME) BEGAN RECORDING IN 1954. IN 1957 SHE HAD A CROSSOVER HIT WITH 'WALKING AFTER MIDNIGHT' AFTER WINNING A TALENT SHOW CONTEST ON CBS.

Patsy joined the Grand Ole Opry in 1961, the same year she recorded 'I Fall To Pieces,' her first Number 1 record. Patsy's 1961 recording of Willie Nelson's composition 'Crazy' became the third of her ten crossover hits and her most popular record. 'She's Got You' (1962) was her last Number 1. The next year, while returning from a benefit show with two other Opry stars, she was killed in an airplane crash.

Cline's music endures more than three decades after her death. Dottie West and Loretta Lynn were friends, fans and contemporaries of Patsy's. Lynn recorded a 1977 album in tribute to her mentor and named her daughter Patsy after her. Reba McEntire and Sylvia Hutton cite Cline as having influenced their musical styles.

In 1973 Patsy was inducted into the Country Music Hall of Fame, and *Sweet Dreams*, a major motion picture loosely based on Cline's life, titled after a posthumously-released hit of Patsy's, was produced in 1985. In 1992 Cline was honored with a special exhibit honoring her memory at the Grand Ole

GEORGE JONES

The Possum

✪ ✪ ✪

Singer/Guitarist
Born: September 12, 1931, Saratoga, Texas

George Jones: there are many imitators, but only one original singer's singer.

George Glenn Jones (called Glenn as a child) began his professional career as a teenager when he sang on an afternoon program on KTXJ Radio in Jasper, Texas.

George moved on to Beaumont, Texas, working on the radio there and in local clubs. After war service with the Marines in Korea, he came back to Beaumont and painted houses by day while singing and playing guitar in clubs in the evening. In 1954 he was discovered and signed to a Beaumont-based record label. Jones next appeared on KNUZ Radio's *Houston Jamboree* and worked as a disc jockey at Beaumont's KTRM Radio where he was nicknamed "the Possum." Recording for Starday Records in Houston, he had his first hit, 'Why Baby Why,' in 1955. George appeared on the *Louisiana Hayride* in 1956 and continued to have Top 10 hits until 1959 when he had his first Number 1 record: his signature song 'White Lightning.'

Jones has had a steady string of solo singles and scores of albums (several of which have gone gold or platinum) into the Nineties. He has also had several duet partners, including Brenda Carter, Ray Charles, Lacy J. Dalton, Merle Haggard, Jeanette Hicks, Johnny Paycheck, Brenda Lee, Shelby Lynne, Melba Montgomery, Gene Pitney, Margie Singleton, and even his stepdaughter Tina. But George's best-remembered duet partner is his ex-wife Tammy Wynette, with whom he recorded 13 duets between 1971 and 1980, three of which ('We're Gonna Hold On,' 'Golden Ring,' and 'Near You') were Number 1 records.

Jones, a Grand Ole Opry member and Grammy Award winner, is often called "the singer's singer" and was inducted into the Country Music Hall of Fame in 1992.

LORETTA LYNN

The Coal Miner's Daughter

✦ ✦ ✦

Singer/Songwriter/Author
Born: April 14, 1935, Butcher's Hollow, Kentucky

Loretta Webb, as she was known before she married Oliver Lynn, really is the coal miner's daughter she sings of in her signature song. Her father worked at the Consolidated Coal Company in Van Lear, Kentucky, 5 miles from "Butcher Holler," as Lynn calls her home town.

The second of Clara and Melvin "Ted" Webb's eight children, Loretta began singing on the family's porch while still a child. Three months before her fourteenth birthday, Loretta married Oliver Lynn, whom she calls by his childhood nickname, "Doolittle" or "Doo," but whom most others call "Mooney," because he used to be a moonshine runner. The couple moved to Custer, Washington and when, she was still only 14, Loretta became pregnant with the first of her six children. For her eighteenth birthday Mooney bought Loretta a Harmony guitar and by 1960 she was entertaining at the Delta Grange Hall. Moving on to Bill's Tavern, where she played for $5 a night, Loretta formed a three-piece band, Loretta's Trailblazers, fronted by her brother Jackie, now known professionally as Jay Lee Webb.

Next the Lynns went to Tacoma, Washington where Mooney got Loretta on Buck Owens' television show, which was shown in Vancouver, British Columbia. A wealthy Vancouver lumber businessman saw the show, contacted the Lynns and signed Loretta to his Zero Records label.

Loretta recorded her own composition, 'Honky Tonk Girl,' in Los Angeles and she and Zero found themselves with a hit on their hands, as the single peaked at Number 14 on the *Billboard* country chart during the summer of 1960. At this time the Lynns were briefly in the record promotion business, traveling to radio stations in their 1955 Ford, urging the DJs to play Loretta's record.

In 1961 they moved to Nashville following Loretta's guest appearance on the Grand Ole Opry the previous October. Teddy and Doyle Wilburn then signed her to their publishing company and brought her to the label for which they recorded, Decca Records.

In 1962 Lynn had her first Top 10 hit, 'Success,' during what was an exciting period for her. She was touring with the Wilburn Brothers who won new fans for her by making Lynn a part of their nationally-

Loretta Lynn was one of country music's feminist lyricists before she even realized it herself.

syndicated television show. Lynn became a Grand Ole Opry member in 1962.

Two years later, Loretta became a 29-year-old grandmother when her daughter, Betty, a teenage bride just like her mother, gave birth to a daughter of her own.

In 1966 Loretta had her first Number 1 record, 'Don't Come Home A Drinkin' (With Lovin' On Your Mind).' Loretta's other solo Number 1 hits include 'Fist City,' 'Woman Of The World (Leave My World Alone),' 'Coal Miner's Daughter,' 'One's On The Way,' 'Rated X,' 'Love Is The Foundation,' 'Trouble In Paradise,' 'Somebody Somewhere (Don't Know What He's Missin' Tonight),' 'She's Got You' (a remake of the Patsy Cline classic) and 'Out Of My Head And Back In My Bed.'

Loretta recorded four duets with Ernest Tubb between 1964 and 1969, but her most memorable are the 14 she recorded with Conway Twitty that charted between 1971 and 1981. Of these, the first five ('After The Fire Is Gone,' 'Lead Me On,' 'Louisiana Woman, Mississippi Man,' 'As Soon As I Hang Up The Phone' and 'Feelin's') were consecutive Number 1 hits!

In 1972 Loretta helped to establish the first International Country Music Fan Fair in Nashville, aided by her fan club presidents, Loudilla, Loretta and Kay Johnson (the Johnson Girls, as Loretta calls them, also preside over the International Fan Club Organization—IFCO), Nashville music executive Irving Waugh, Bill Anderson, George Hamilton IV and Country Music Association officials.

A Grammy Award-winner, Loretta titled her 1976 autobiography *Coal Miner's Daughter.* A best-seller, the book was made into an Academy Awarding-winning feature film starring Cissy Spacek as Loretta in 1980. In 1972 Loretta became the first woman Country Music Association Entertainer of the Year, and in 1988 she was inducted into the Country Music Hall of Fame.

MINNIE PEARL

Cousin Minnie

✪ ✪ ✪

Comedienne/Recording Artist/Author
Born: October 25, 1912, Centreville, Tennessee

THE FIFTH DAUGHTER OF THOMAS AND FANNIE COLLIE, SARAH OPHELIA COLLIE MADE HER FIRST PUBLIC APPEARANCE AT THE AGE OF 18 MONTHS WHEN SHE SANG AT A RECITAL PUT ON BY HER SISTERS' PIANO TEACHER. AT THE AGE OF 6 SHE WAS SINGING AND PLAYING PIANO AT FIRST WORLD WAR BOND RALLIES.

Collie studied dramatics at Hickman County High School, graduating from Nashville's Ward-Belmont finishing school (now Belmont University) in stage technique in 1932. At that stage a career in country comedy was the farthest thing from her mind, Ophelia's main ambition being to become a dancer. Her first job was drama coach at Atlanta, Georgia's Wayne P. Sewell Production Company where she trained other prospective drama coaches.

Ophelia spent 6 years with the Sewell Company, representing it on the road, and it was during her travels directing amateur plays for local schools that she appeared on stage herself, singing silly songs and delivering monologues that convinced her she had a future in comedy.

While touring Baileytown, Alabama, Ophelia met a mountain woman who became the inspiration for her *alter ego*, Minnie Pearl, a character who came to life following an engagement Ophelia played in Aiken, South Carolina in 1939. Ophelia experimented for quite some time refining the persona. "Minnie" and "Pearl" were popular first names among southern women during the Thirties. Grinders Switch, Minnie's hometown, is the name of a tiny crossroads community near Centreville, Tennessee.

By 1940 the Cousin Minnie Pearl character had fully taken shape. The familiar spinster wearing the flower-bedecked dime-store straw hat with the dangling price tag and a frilly country-girl dress was becoming a comedy sensation as she screeched her "How-dee!" greeting to her audiences. Impressed with Minnie's following (Collie came to be addressed as Minnie), the Grand Ole Opry asked her to make a guest appearance. Minnie's début before the Opry's national radio audience was a great success, resulting in her being invited to join the Opry in 1940. Audiences loved Minnie and her monologues about her mythical family: Brother Hezzie, Uncle Nabob and Aunt Brozie.

On February 23, 1947, Ophelia married pilot Henry Cannon, whom she had met the previous year. That same year the comedienne appeared on the first country music show ever to play in New York's famed Carnegie Hall. Ski-nosed comedian Rod Brasfield often joined Minnie on the Opry, trading quips and anecdotes. Minnie set Rod up with the straight lines so she could be sure to get all the laughs.

During the Fifties and Sixties, when Minnie was not on the Opry she appeared at supper clubs and theatres, at state and county fairs and auditoriums across the United States. During 1966 she had her first and only chart record, a Top 10 hit called 'Giddyup Go-Answer' (the "response" to Red Sovine's Number 1 hit of the same year, 'Giddyup Go').

Minnie appeared on network variety shows and

Minnie Pearl: "The Queen of Country Comedy."

was one of the original cast members of the TV series Hee Haw. She was inducted into the Country Music Hall of Fame in 1975 and her autobiography, Minnie Pearl, was published in 1980. Opryland's Minnie Pearl Museum contains excerpts from many of Minnie's televised appearances as well as artifacts and memorabilia from her long professional career.

Sarah Cannon, as she is also known, received the American Cancer Society's Courage Award in 1987 following her double mastectomy 2 years earlier. She had used her operation as an opportunity to publicize the importance of mammography. The Sarah Cannon Cancer Center, a part of Nashville's Centennial Medical Center, was established in her honor.

Minnie Pearl was for many years a neighbor of Tennessee's governors, living next door to the Governors' Mansion on South Curtiswood Lane in Nashville. In June 1991 she suffered a stroke and moved into Nashville's Richland Place Retirement Center.

KITTY WELLS

The Queen of Country Music

❁ ❁ ❁

Singer/Guitarist
Born: August 30, 1919, Nashville, Tennessee

Muriel Ellen Deason grew up singing gospel songs at church. At the age of 14 Muriel learned to play guitar and at 15 she was playing at local dances. At 16 she began singing on Nashville's WSIX Radio *Dixie Early Birds Show*. There she met her husband-to-be, Johnny Wright. The couple married on October 30, 1937 and it wasn't long before Kitty Wells (the stage name comes from the folk song 'Sweet Kitty Wells') became a featured part of the newly formed Johnny and Jack (Anglin) Show. The musical organization also included a back-up band: the Tennessee Mountain Boys.

Touring extensively during the Thirties and Forties, the Johnny And Jack Show received increased radio exposure in 1940 when they appeared on Greensboro, North Carolina's WBIG Radio, before moving on to Knoxville's WNOX Radio *Midday Merry Go Round*.

In 1947, when Johnny And Jack joined the Grand Ole Opry, Kitty (still their featured singer) went along with them. Their Opry stay was a brief one. Johnny, Jack and Kitty moved on to Shreveport, Louisiana's KWKH Radio where they became stars on the newly formed *Louisiana Hayride*. After 5 years on the *Hayride*, Johnny, Jack and Kitty received an offer to rejoin the Grand Ole Opry in 1952.

In the same year Kitty also received a recording contract from Decca Records. When she had signed her previous contract—with RCA Records, in 1949—the record-buying public had shown little interest in the recordings of female country singers. But now things had changed. Her new contract enabled her to come out from the shadows of the Johnny And Jack Show and become the first female to reach Number 1 on the country music charts!

Part of Kitty's good fortune was due to the strength of the song she recorded, J. D. Miller's composition, 'It Wasn't God Who Made Honky-Tonk Angels.' An "answer," or response, song, Wells' record contradicted the message of Hank Thompson's 'The Wild Side Of Life' by suggesting that the waywardness of honky-tonk angels was not divinely engineered but due to the culpability of straying husbands. Wells' crossover hit not only caught the attention of both country and popular music fans; it also made a fan of Hank Williams' songwriting collaborator Fred Rose. He dubbed Kitty Wells "the Queen of Country Music," a title she has retained for more than 40 years.

Kitty followed up the biggest hit of her career with two more answer songs: the 1953 'Paying For That Back Street Affair,' answering Webb Pierce's 'Back Street Affair' and peaking at Number 6 on Billboard's country chart; and then 'Hey Joe,' answering Carl Smith's 'Hey Joe' and reaching Number 8.

During the Fifties and early Sixties, Kitty had several Top 10 hits including 'Makin' Believe,' 'Repenting,' 'Mommy For A Day,' 'Three Ways (To Love You)' and 'Left To Right,' before having her only other Number 1 solo hit with 'Heartbreak USA' in 1961.

Her solo success continued up to 1979. Over the years Kitty cut a number of duets, beginning in 1954 when she and Red Foley had a

Number 1 record with 'One by One.' Staying for 41 weeks on Billboard's country music chart, that recording holds a chart longevity record for a country duo.

Foley and Wells' follow-up duet, 'I'm A Stranger In My Home,' also released in 1954, reached Number 12 on Billboard. Kitty and Red charted with eight other duets between 1955 and 1969. Wells and Webb Pierce had three duets—'Oh, So Many Years,' 'One Week Later' and 'Finally'—between 1957 and 1964.

Kitty's other duet partners have been Grand Ole Opry star Roy Drusky (with whom she recorded 'I Can't Tell My Heart That' in 1960), Johnny Wright ('We'll Stick Together,' 1968) and Rayburn

Kitty Wells: the "girl" who put the "boys" on notice.

Anthony ('The Wild Side Of Life,' 1979).

Kitty, who was inducted into the Country Music Hall of Fame in 1976, received the Grammy Lifetime Achievement Award in 1991. She and her husband oversee the Kitty Wells/Johnny Wright Family Country Junction Museum, a favorite Nashville area tourist attraction.

HANK WILLIAMS

Luke the Drifter

❂ ❂ ❂

Singer/Songwriter/Guitarist
Born: September 17, 1923, Mount Olive, Alabama
Died: January 1, 1953, *en route* to Canton, Ohio

Hiram King Williams, born just outside Georgiana, Alabama, 60 miles from Montgomery, began singing in the church choir when he was 6 years old. When he was 7, his father, Shelton, a shell-shocked First World War veteran, checked himself into a veteran's hospital, leaving Hank virtually fatherless.

His mother, Lilly, the church organist, gave her 7-year-old son a $3.50 guitar which Hank was taught to play by Rufe Payne, an elderly black Montgomery street musician known to his young pupil as Tee-Tot. Discouraging mimicry, Payne taught Hank to sing the blues with authentic emotion.

At the age of 12, Williams took what he had learned from his mentor and made his professional singing début during a Montgomery amateur contest. He sang 'The WPA Blues' and won $15. By the late Thirties he had made Montgomery his home, shining shoes and selling peanuts on the street. When he was 15 he formed his Drifting Cowboys band. Hank And The Drifting Cowboys played on Montgomery's WSFA Radio for over a decade.

In 1946 Hank began his recording career on Sterling Records, but it wasn't until 1947, having signed with the newly formed MGM Records, that he had his first success when 'Move It On Over' reached Number 4 in *Billboard*. Williams obtained his MGM recording contract with the help of former tin-pan alley songwriter-turned-Nashville music publisher Fred Rose. Rose not only masterminded Hank's recordings, arranging the music and playing on and producing the sessions; he also helped Hank with his songwriting and directed his career, threatened at times by Hank's severe back problems and his alcoholism. (Hank's son says that his father was well on the way to alcoholism when he was as young as 15 because of all the honky-tonks he played in.)

In 1948 Hank had two more hit records, 'Honky Tonkin'' and 'I'm A Long Gone Daddy'. In 1949, following his first Number 1 record, 'Lovesick Blues,' a song first popularized in 1925 by yodeler Emmett Miller, he was booked as a regular on KWKH Radio's *Louisiana Hayride*. Williams joined the Grand Ole Opry in 1949, and in the Fifties recorded songs using the pseudonym Luke the Drifter.

The late Opry star Doyle Wilburn, who met Hank on the *Louisiana Hayride*, recalled Williams as a man fascinated with pinball machines and as an entertainer who honored his commitments. Even after the success of 'Lovesick Blues,' he faithfully fulfilled all the one-room schoolhouse contracts he had signed before hitting the big time.

Vic Willis, one of the Oklahoma Wranglers back in 1946, recalls

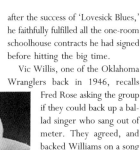

Fred Rose asking the group if they could back up a ballad singer who sang out of meter. They agreed, and backed Williams on a song called 'Wealth Won't Save Your Poor Wicked Soul.' It seems Hank had trouble pronouncing the word "poor." Following several failed attempts to get it right, the song was released in 1947, with Williams' unusual diction reluctantly preserved for posterity.

While at the Opry Hank continued to have hits like 'Wedding Bells,' 'Mind Your Own Business,' 'You're Gonna Change' and 'My Bucket's Got A

Hank Williams' diction may have been unusual, but his songs will endure.

Hole In It.' Several others—'Long Gone Lonesome Blues,' 'Why Don't You Love Me,' 'Hey Good Lookin'' and 'Jambalaya (On The Bayou)'—were Number 1 records. But Williams' demise was foreshadowed when he was fired from the Grand Ole Opry in 1952. He had his last Number 1 during his lifetime with the ironically-titled 'I'll Never Get Out Of This World Alive.'

Hank Williams died *en route* to a booking in Canton, Ohio on New Year's Day 1953, supposedly from a heart attack brought on by excessive drinking. After his death his records continued to sell. Three—'Kaw-Liga,' 'Your Cheatin' Heart' and 'Take These Chains From My Heart'—went to Number 1 in 1953. His reissued recordings continued to chart as late as 1976.

In 1961 Hank Williams was one of the first three artists to be posthumously inducted into the Country Music Hall of Fame. In 1964 George Hamilton starred in *Your Cheatin' Heart*, a movie loosely based on Hank Williams's life, with a soundtrack by Hank Williams, Jr.

EDDY ARNOLD

LAST OF THE LOVE SONG SINGERS: THEN AND NOW
RCA, 1993

I
N THE BOOKLET WHICH ACCOMPANIES THIS BOXED SET OF 27 RECORDINGS, EDDY ARNOLD WRITES THAT, AS HIS music indicates, he is a sentimentalist. The "Then And Now" refers to the two discs found here. The first is a selection of 16 previously-released hits, including 'I Really Don't Want To Know,' Arnold's favorite of all his recorded songs

'Cattle Call,' was originally written by Tex Owens, but Eddy notes that Fred Rose retooled it and that it is Rose's version that is familiar to Arnold's fans. Arnold credits his 1965 recording of Hank Cochran's 'Make The World Go Away' with reviving his career, as his record sales had fallen off prior to its release.

Cindy Walker is the principal writer of 'You Don't Know Me,' but Eddy, her co-writer, supplied her with the title which inspired the story line. He admits the song is loosely autobiographical.

Bill Anderson wrote and Chet Atkins produced Eddy's 'The Tip Of My Fingers.' 'What's He Doin' In My World' is notable because it is the first of the "world" songs that Arnold popularized during the Sixties. 'That's How Much I Love You,' which Eddy wrote with Wally Fowler and J. Graydon Hall, was Arnold's first hit, in 1946. Arnold praises John D. Loudermilk's composition, 'Then You Can Tell Me Goodbye' as a well-written song. Eddy's recordings of Bob Montgomery's composition, 'Misty Blue,' 'They Don't Make Love Like They Used To,' and 'Lonely Again' round out the "Then" collection.

The "Now" disc contains the title song—a Wayne Carson composition—eight other new songs and two not-so-new songs: 'When The Wind Blows In Chicago' and Fred Rose's 'Afraid.'

GARTH BROOKS

NO FENCES
Liberty, 1990

garth brooks
NO FENCES

By THE TIME GARTH BROOKS' SECOND ALBUM *NO FENCES* WAS RELEASED, HE WAS NO LONGER BEING VIEWED as Clint Black's rival. Virtually every country fan knew who Brooks was and his crossover appeal was making country music "cool" again.

Many wondered how Brooks could follow up such classics from his first album as 'If Tomorrow Never Comes' and 'The Dance,' but the singer, who also included a cover of the Jim Reeves classic 'I Know One' on the first LP, was out to prove both the strength of today's music and the enduring appeal of a country classic rendered with total sincerity.

No Fences, as the title implies, confirms Brooks' lack of musical boundaries and an acceptance of that fact by both country fans, who

brought it to the top of *Billboard*'s country album chart following its début on September 29, 1990, and by pop fans, who took it to Number 12 on *Billboard*'s pop chart.

No Fences is the album containing the 'The Thunder Rolls,' the song which inspired the music video of the same name that was banned by The Nashville Network because of its graphic scenes of sexual infidelity and spousal abuse. The album also includes 'Two Of A Kind,' 'Workin' On A Full House' (the antithesis of 'The Thunder Rolls'), the blue-collar anthem 'Friends In Low Places,' the message of hope in 'Unanswered Prayers,' and 'Wolves,' written by Brooks' protégée, Stephanie Davis.

GLEN CAMPBELL

THE BEST OF GLEN CAMPBELL
Liberty, 1987

FIRST OUT IN ALBUM FORM IN 1976, THIS DISC, WHICH REMAINED ON BILLBOARD'S COUNTRY ALBUM CHART FOR 23 WEEKS, contains much of Glen's most enduring music.

Leading off with Larry Weiss' well-known 'Rhinestone Cowboy'—which Campbell decided to record having heard Weiss' version on the radio—Glen moves on to John Hartford's 'Gentle On My Mind,' the full-length version of *The Glen Campbell Goodtime Hour* theme song.

Jimmy Webb, the songwriter most associated with Glen Campbell's early hits, has contributed three hits to this CD: 'Wichita Lineman,' 'Galveston' and 'By The Time I Get To Phoenix,' as well as the lesser-known 'The Moon Is A Mistress.'

Also found here is David Paich's 'Houston (I'm Comin' To See You)', not to be confused with at least two other unrelated compositions about the Texas city recorded by Dean Martin and Larry Gatlin And The Gatlin Brothers Band.

Other selections are 'Country Boy (You've Got Your Feet In L.A.),' Gordon Lightfoot's ballad, 'The Last Time I Saw Her,' the inspirational, upbeat 'Try A Little Kindness,' Glen's convincing cover of the late Conway Twitty's 'It's Only Make Believe' and the pointed 'I Knew Jesus (Before He Was A Superstar).'

An interesting sidelight is that Kenny Rogers, who in recent years has become famous for his passion for photography through publishing photos of his celebrity friends in book form, is given photo credit for the pictures adorning the front and back of the original vinyl album *The Best Of Glen Campbell*, duplicated on this compact disc.

JOHNNY CASH

THE ESSENTIAL JOHNNY CASH: 1955–1983
Columbia, 1992

THIS THREE-DISC BOX SET OF 75 DIGITALLY-REMASTERED CASH CLASSICS CONTAINS A BOOKLET WITH LINER NOTES AND historic photos covering the most prolific years of Cash's nearly 40-year-long career. Cash wrote or co-wrote no less than 21 of the 29 songs on the first disc, including 'Hey Porter,' 'Cry, Cry, Cry,' 'Folsom Prison Blues,' 'Get Rhythm,' 'I Walk The Line,' 'Home Of The Blues,' 'Give My Love To Rose,' 'Rock Island Line,' 'Big River,' 'Oh, What A Dream,' 'What Do I Care,' 'All Over Again,' 'I Still Miss Someone,' 'Walking The Blues,' 'Frankie's Man Johnny,' 'Tennessee Flat-Top Box,' 'Sing It Pretty, Sue,' 'Pickin' Time' and

'Five Feet High And Rising.' The first 15 cuts on the first disc were recorded during Cash's stint at Sun Records.

Johnny wrote or co-wrote only seven of the 23 songs on disc two: 'Don't Take Your Guns To Town,' 'The Big Battle,' 'The Legend Of John Henry's Hammer,' 'I Got Stripes,' 'Understand Your Man,' 'See Ruby Fall' and 'Cisco Clifton's Fillin' Station.'

The third disc's 23 selections include live versions of Cash's 'Folsom Prison Blues,' 'Cocaine Blues' and 'San Quentin' as well as Shel Silverstein's 'A Boy Named Sue.' Other Cash compositions are 'Singin' In Viet Nam Talkin' Blues,' 'What Is Truth,' 'Flesh And Blood,' 'Hit The Road And Go,' 'Rockabilly Blues (Texas 1955),' 'I Will Rock And Roll With You,' 'After The Ball' and 'I'm Gonna Sit On The Porch And Pick On My Old Guitar.'

The remaining tracks are by artists such as Bob Dylan, Kris Kristofferson, Jerry Chesnut, Mick Jagger and Keith Richards, Stan Jones and Rodney Crowell.

ROSANNE CASH

ROSANNE CASH HITS 1979–1989
CBS, 1989

THIS COMPACT DISC OFFERS 12 OF ROSANNE'S MOST COMMERCIAL SONGS, ALL BUT ONE EITHER PRODUCED OR CO-produced by her ex-husband, Rodney Crowell. It leads off with Rosanne's self-penned 'Seven Year Ache.' Recorded in 1980, this song, about the proverbial marital itch, is arguably her best "attitude" number. It is followed by her August 1988 remake of the Beatles' 'I Don't Want To Spoil The Party.' After this comes Rosanne's composition 'Hold On,' recorded in April, 1984 in New York City.

'Blue Moon With Heartache,' another Cash composition and produced by Crowell, is from the 1980 sessions at Davlin Sound in North Hollywood, California, while 'My Baby Thinks He's A Train,' written by Leroy Preston, was produced at North Hollywood's Magnolia Sound in August, 1980. 'No Memories Hangin' Round,' written and produced by Rodney Crowell, was recorded in Los Angeles in March, 1979.

David Malloy produced 'I Don't Know Why You Don't Want Me.' Co-written by Rosanne and Rodney, the song, recorded in Nashville in April, 1984 was inspired by Cash's frustration at her artistry failing to win industry recognition and awards. 'I Wonder' was written by Larry Preston and recorded in Nashville in November, 1981.

Rosanne recorded Benmont Tench and Tom Petty's 'Never Be You' in December, 1984 in New York City. John Hiatt wrote Rosanne's recording of 'The Way We Mend A Broken Heart,' recorded in Nashville in March, 1987, as was her remake of her father's composition, 'Tennessee Flat Top Box.' Cash remembered 'Tennessee Flat Top Box' as being one of her father's hits, but until she recorded it, she thought the song was in the public domain.

Ironically, while Johnny's recording peaked at Number 11 in 1962, Rosanne's version reached the Number 1 position on *Billboard*'s country chart in 1988.

The compact disc is rounded out by Rosanne and Rodney's co-production of Preston Smith's composition, 'Black and White.' This, together with 'I Don't Want To Spoil The Party,' were recorded at the same session in 1988 and are the album's only previously unreleased songs. Musicians Mark O'Connor, Ricky Skaggs and Billy Joe Walker, Jr contributed to this session, as did vocalists Bobby Bare, Emmylou Harris, Vince Gill, John Cowan and Rodney Crowell.

PATSY CLINE

PATSY CLINE LIVE VOLUME TWO
MCA, 1989

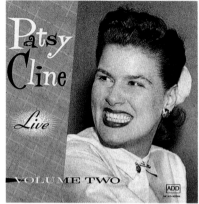

A SUPPLEMENT TO PATSY CLINE LIVE AT THE OPRY AND RELEASED IN 1988, PATSY CLINE LIVE VOLUME TWO CONTAINS 12 recordings of Patsy's Opry performances that had not been heard since they were originally broadcast between 1956 and 1962. Though none of these cuts, recorded between 1956 and 1960 (only seven of them commercially), was a hit for Patsy, they are rare excerpts from military recruitment radio shows.

The applause tracks heard on the songs from the 1956 shows—Sammy Masters' 'Turn The Cards Slowly,' Webb Pierce's 'Yes, I Know Why,' Pappy Stewart's 'Come On In And Make Yourself At Home,' Stan Lebowsky and Herb Newman's 'The Wayward Wind,' Jimmie Loden and Jack Morrow's

'For Rent,' and George London's 'Stop, Look and Listen'—are misleading for, as noted earlier, these songs were not performed before live audiences. Rather, they were studio cuts originally intended for subsequent radio broadcast.

Transcribed on to 16-in. discs, the 12 performances were excerpted from three 15-minute series: the US Air Force's Country Music Time, the Army's Country Style USA and the American Navy's Country Hoedown. Faron Young served as host during Patsy's two Country Hoedown appearances, and her band, the Country Deputies, were among the musicians backing Cline on the three songs she sang in each broadcast.

When Patsy hosted Country Style USA in June 1960, she sang her version of Roger Miller's composition 'When A House Is Not A Home.' Making a return appearance to the program 3 months later, Cline

reprised Connie Francis' 1958 pop hit, 'Stupid Cupid.' In 1961 Patsy hosted Country Music Time, singing the popular music classic, 'Side By Side' and Red Foley's gospel standard, 'Just A Closer Walk With Thee.'

During the winter of 1962, Cline returned to Country Music Time, performing 'Strange' (the flip side of her hit 'She's Got You') and a Hank Cochran–Velma Smith composition, 'Shoes.' The digital remastering process has restored to their original clarity these recordings by the first woman inducted into the Country Music Hall of Fame.

LEFTY FRIZZELL

AMERICAN ORIGINALS
Columbia, 1990

A S IS THE CASE WITH COLUMBIA'S ISSUES OF *AMERICAN ORIGINALS* TITLES ON SONNY JAMES, GEORGE Morgan and others, some of Frizzell's songs one might have expected to find on this compilation are glaringly absent, while others, like 'She's Gone, Gone, Gone' which was never a hit for Lefty, are included. That said, generations of country music stars influenced by his music will argue that Frizzell could take any song and make it his own with his inimitable phrasing.

The ten juke-box favorites on this compact disc represent the most successful years of Lefty's 22-year-long honky-tonkin' stint at Columbia Records. Leading off with his 1964 recording of 'Saginaw, Michigan' (his last Number 1 single), the album continues with one of the seven hits with which Lefty dominated the embryonic 1951 country charts. After that comes Frizzell's definitive recording of 'Mom And Dad's Waltz.' Lefty's classic rendering of his own composition precedes Patti Page's cover version by a decade. Frizzell's record became a Number 2 country record for 8 consecutive weeks in 1951.

This collection would be incomplete without Lefty's haunting 1959 treatment of Marijohn Willkin and Danny Dill's standard, 'The Long Black Veil.' Other country stars have also recorded this tale of murder and grief, but it is Frizzell's compelling performance that endures.

Side Two begins with Harlan Howard's 'Gone, Gone, Gone,' followed by another of Lefty's four 1951 Number 1 releases, 'Always Late (With Your Kisses).' Frizzell's own composition, 'I Want To Be With You Always,' began his 1951 streak. Country fans kept the song at Number 1 for 11 weeks. 'Forever (And Always),' co-written by Lefty and a Number 6 hit for him in 1952, rounds out *American Originals*.

TOM T. HALL

TOM T. HALL'S GREATEST HITS
Mercury, 1972

T HE ONLY ONE OF TOM T. HALL'S ALBUMS CURRENTLY FOUND ON COMPACT DISC, THIS GREATEST HITS PACKAGE REMAINED on *Billboard*'s country album chart for 13 weeks following its original release on vinyl. Like most of Hall's music, 'Homecoming' is based on a true story. This one is about Tom's trying to explain his lifestyle to his father, his neglect of family and friends, and the pretense that goes along with the hard work in a country music career. Hall didn't really meet the 'Shoeshine Man' in Montgomery, Alabama as the song's narration indicates, but despite this and other liberties Tom takes, the song still rings true.

'I Miss A Lot Of Trains' is little more than filler material and could easily have been replaced with any number of songs that Tom wrote which outshine his hits and yet remain overlooked, such as 'The Hitch-hiker' or 'That'll Be All Right With Me.' 'Salute To A Switchblade' was inspired by Hall's 3 years in the army, and 'The Ballad Of Forty Dollars' by an earlier period in his life when he worked in a cemetery.

'I Washed My Face In The Morning Dew,' culled from an old expression, is the title of Hall's first hit, in 1967, while 'That's How I Got To Memphis' missed the charts but has been revived by Bobby Bare and Rosanne Cash. 'The Year That Clayton Delaney Died' is a tribute to Tom's childhood hero Lonnie Easterling, the teenage leader of a five-piece country band. 'A Week In A Country Jail' resulted from a drunk driving citation.

'One Hundred Children' lauds the world's bravest children who are pleading with political leaders to leave them an environmentally safe world, and 'Me And Jesus,' inspired by a favorite expression of Tom's late mother, Della Lena Hall, is an affirmation of religious simplicity.

WAYLON JENNINGS

THE BEST OF WAYLON JENNINGS
RCA, 1970

OPENING WITH A REAL TEAR-JERKER, 'THE DAYS OF SAND AND SHOVELS,' A TOP 20 COUNTRY RECORD FOR WAYLON (and a pop hit for Bobby Vinton) in 1969, Waylon (with vocal accompaniment by the Kimberlys) croons his 1969 country cover of Richard Harris' 1968 pop hit, 'MacArthur Park.' Jennings' version of the Jimmy Webb composition crossed over but barely charted pop.

Another pre-"outlaw" period hit for Waylon, 'Delia's Gone,' co-written by Jennings and his brother Tommy, also grazed the pop charts, while his release of the compelling 'Walk On Out Of My Mind' became his first Top 5 hit in 1968. Side One closes with Waylon's 1968 hit, the gentle plea for realism, 'Anita, You're Dreaming,'

which Jennings co-wrote with Don Bowman. Side Two opens with 'Only Daddy That'll Walk The Line,' a Number 2 record for 5 consecutive weeks in 1968 and Waylon's highest charting recording prior to 1974. That spirited song and 'Just To Satisfy You' (another Jennings-Bowman collaboration) which follows, are the only two songs in this collection that endure as part of Jennings' present-day concert performances. 'I Got You,' Waylon's 1968 duet with Anita Carter, peaked at Number 4 that year, while the plaintive 'Something's Wrong In California' was a Top 20 hit for Jennings in 1969.

This "best of" collection closes with Waylon's recording of Mel Tillis' composition, 'Ruby, Don't Take Your Love To Town.' Hardly one of Jennings' greatest hits (it failed to reach the charts), his interpretation is nevertheless every bit as convincing as the definitive Kenny Rogers And The First Edition's 1969 hit or other recordings of the song by Tillis, Johnny Darrell, and countless others.

GEORGE JONES

THE BEST OF GEORGE JONES 1955–1967
Rhino, 1991

THE BEST OF GEORGE JONES
1955-1967

JONES' EARLIEST YEARS ARE REPRESENTED BY 18 TRACKS, FOUR OF WHICH—GEORGE'S DUET WITH GENE PITNEY, 'I'VE GOT Five Dollars And It's Saturday Night,' 'Love Bug,' 'I'm A People' and 'Walk Through This World With Me'—are CD bonus tracks.

Many of the Jones classics one would expect to find are here, such as three of George's first five 1956 Starday hits: 'Why, Baby, Why,' 'What Am I Worth?' and 'Just One More.' 'Don't Stop The Music' (1957) is the first of Jones' Mercury recordings. Others are 'Color Of The Blues' (1958), 1959's 'White Lightning,' the 1960 tale of marital betrayal 'The Window Up Above,' George's second Number 1 record 'Tender Years' (1961) and his

Top 5 recording in 1962 'Aching Breaking Heart.'

George moved from Mercury to United Artists where, also in 1962, he had his third Number 1 hit, 'She Thinks I Still Care,' and a Top 5 recording, 'The Girl I Used To Know.' The next year Jones and Melba Montgomery's duet 'We Must Have Been Out Of Our Minds' peaked at Number 3, while George had a Top 5 hit with 'You Comb Her Hair.'

Jones' 1963 recording of 'The Race Is On,' written by Don Rollins following a visit to a Phoenix, Arizona racetrack, preceded singer Jack Jones' 1965 hit as well as Sawyer Brown's 1990 cover.

GEORGE JONES AND TAMMY WYNETTE

GREATEST HITS
Epic, 1977

THIS COLLECTION OF TEN BILLY SHERILL PRODUCTIONS PLAYS OUT THE SAGA OF THE JONES–WYNETTE MARRIAGE AND divorce in song and remained on *Billboard*'s country album chart for 20 weeks.

'Golden Rings', a Number 1 hit for George and Tammy in 1976, chronicles the birth and death of a marriage. It remained on the charts for 17 weeks, longer than any of Jones and Wynette's other duets. It is followed by the couple's first Number 1 duet, 1973's affirmation of marital fidelity, 'We're Gonna Hold On.' 'We Loved It Away' was a similarly optimistic 1974 Top 10 release, while 'Take Me,' released in 1971, and 'Near You,' which débuted in 1976, are dreamy declarations of love.

Side Two kicks off with 'Southern California,' the 1977 story, complete with soliloquies, of a couple's wistful but futile attempt to bridge their differences. 'God's Gonna Get'cha (For That)' is a handclappin' gospel-flavored moralistic warning from 1975, while '(We're Not) The Jet Set' is Jones and Wynette's cleverly written but not-too-convincing attempt to persuade people that they are basically "just folks."

'Let's Build A World Together,' a 1973 ballad, relies heavily on Billy Sherrill's production techniques, often criticized as being overpowering.

The album closes with 'The Ceremony,' a poignant or pointless (depending upon your outlook) reprise of what listeners are intended to believe approximates to the couple's thoughts as they repeat wedding vows set to music. Nothing is left to the imagination, including the preacher's words. The song was released in 1972.

KRIS KRISTOFFERSON

ME AND BOBBY MCGEE
CBS, 1988

THIS ALBUM MARKS KRIS KRISTOFFERSON'S DÉBUT AS A RELUCTANT RECORDING ARTIST. NOTING THE ROUGH EDGES ON some of the tracks, Kristofferson downplays as a demo what is arguably his best work, recorded 2 years before his first hit as an artist.

Liner notes by Johnny Cash, Kris' mentor, say it all, as do the astounding number of Kristofferson compositions which have stood the test of time. In addition to the title song, which Kris co-wrote with his producer, Fred Foster, three of the earliest Kristofferson-penned hits are here: a jaunty and up-tempo 'Help Me Make It Through The Night,' 'For The Good Times' and 'Sunday Mornin' Comin' Down.'

The other songs are gems too. 'Blame It On The Stones' is a poke at hypocrisy with the concomitant tongue-in-cheek suggestion that all of the world's problems can be laid at the feet of Mick Jagger and friends. 'To Beat The Devil' (also found on *Hello, I'm Johnny Cash*) is Kris' tribute to Cash. The influence of Roger Miller upon Kristofferson's is evidenced by 'The Best Of All Possible Worlds,' a song about a happy-go-lucky drunk in and out of jail. 'The Law Is For Protection Of The People' is a protest song, evoking imagery of the ultimate protester, Jesus. And 'Casey's Last Ride' is a harrowing tale of desperation portended by alcoholism, infidelity and loneliness.

'Just The Other Side Of Nowhere' details a reluctant decision to return home after having nothing to show for the dues the protagonist has paid. 'Darby's Castle' (also found on Bobby Bare's *Bare Country*) is a story of destruction brought on by the communication gap between workaholic Cecil Darby and his cheating wife.

LORETTA AND CONWAY

THE VERY BEST OF LORETTA AND CONWAY
MCA, 1979

T HIS 14-SONG COLLEC-TION, SPANNING LYNN AND TWITTY'S DUETS FROM 1973 TO 1978, WAS ON BILLBOARD'S country album chart for 22 weeks.

The Cajun feel of 'Louisiana Woman, Mississippi Man' changes to the secrecy of 'Love From Seven Til Ten.' 'As Soon As I Pick Up The Phone' is a humorous tale of an impending break-up, while 'You're The Reason Our Kids Are Ugly' is an equally comical approach to the blame game. Next are duet versions of Conway's hits 'It's Only Make Believe' and 'I've Already Loved You In My Mind.'

Side Two features 1971's 'After The Fire Is Gone,' later covered by Willie Nelson and Tracy Nelson, the infectious 'I Can't Love You Enough' and the intense 'Feelin's.' The chemistry between the two is best heard on their remake of Jim Stafford's 1974 hit, 'Spiders And Snakes.'

'The Letter' is a head-scratching tale of a woman asking her old flame's help in making her spouse jealous. 'Lead Me On' is a plea for the proper assumption of responsibility, while 'God Bless America Again,' co-written by Bobby Bare and the late Boyce Hawkins, is a request in the name of patriotism.

WILLIE NELSON

WILLIE NELSON'S GREATEST HITS (AND SOME THAT WILL BE)
Columbia, 1981

F IRST RELEASED IN 1981, THIS 20-SONG COLLECTION WAS ON BILLBOARD'S COUNTRY ALBUM CHART FOR 35 WEEKS.

Contrary to the album's title, 'Railroad Lady,' 'Heartaches Of A Fool,' Lefty Frizzell's 'Look What Thoughts Will Do,' Elvis Presley's 'Heartbreak Hotel' and 'Til I Gain Control Again' were never actually hits for Willie.

Songs that were hits for him include 'Blue Eyes Crying In The Rain,' 'Whiskey River,' Willie's frenzied solo version of 'Good Hearted Woman' (a hit for Waylon Jennings in 1972 and again as a duet by Jennings and Nelson in 1976), Hoagy Carmichael's 'Georgia On My Mind,' 'If You've Got The Money I've Got The Time,' 'Uncloudy Day,' Willie's solo version of Ed Bruce's 'Mamas Don't Let Your Babies Grow Up To Be Cowboys' (another Waylon And Willie hit), 'My Heroes Have Always Been Cowboys,' 'Help Me Make It Through The Night,' 'Angel Flying Too Close To The Ground,' 'I'd Have To Be Crazy,' 'Faded Love' 'On The Road Again' (which is Willie's signature song), 'If You Could Touch Her At All' and 'Stay A Little Longer.'

DOLLY PARTON

BEST OF
DOLLY PARTON
RCA, 1988

FIRST RELEASED IN 1975, THESE SIDES SPENT 26 WEEKS ON *BILLBOARD*'S COUNTRY ALBUM CHART. PRODUCED AND arranged by Porter Wagoner, they show the impact of Wagoner and the role he played in showcasing Dolly's vocals and bringing them to the attention of those not attuned to country music. The marriage of Porter's touch and Dolly's abilities as a songwriter and singer are apparent on the first of these ten cuts, 'Jolene,' a song of a woman fearful of losing her man to a rival.

'Lonely Comin' Down' and the spiritual 'When I Sing For Him' are the only two songs in this collection not written by Parton. 'When I Sing For Him' was never released as a single by Dolly though Keith Bradford charted with it in 1979.

'The Bargain Store,' a Number 1 record for Parton like 'Jolene,' caught fans' attention due to its unusual title and its use of simile. 'Touch Your Woman,' a bit of self-assertion daring for its day (1972) was none the less a Top 10 record for Dolly.

'I Will Always Love You,' a Number 1 record for Parton in 1974, proved its durability when, as part of the soundtrack for the movie *The Best Little Whorehouse In Texas*, it was again a Number 1 for Dolly in 1982, this time crossing over to the pop charts as well. Then, a decade later, Whitney Houston took 'I Will Always Love You'— part of the soundtrack to the motion picture *The Bodyguard*—to the top of the popular music charts. The lilting 'Love Is Like A Butterfly,' the follow-up to 'I Will Always Love You,' was also a Number 1 record for Dolly in 1974. 'Coat Of Many Colors,' Parton's autobiographical account of her childhood, is a song about values, as is her peaceful portrayal of 'My Tennessee Mountain Home,' made in 1973.

JIM REEVES

THE BEST OF
JIM REEVES
RCA, 1992

THIS FIRST IN A SERIES OF "BEST OF JIM" VOLUMES RELEASED IN ALBUM FORM DURING THE LATE SEVENTIES REMAINED ON *Billboard*'s country album chart for 41 weeks. It leads off with 'He'll Have To Go,' which was not only Reeves' signature song, but his biggest record. Released in December 1959, it peaked at Number 2 on *Billboard*'s pop chart and was Number 1 on *Billboard*'s country chart for 14 out of 34 chart weeks.

The follow-up to 'He'll Have to Go'—'I'm Getting Better'—was another crossover hit for Jim in 1960. His 1961 recording of Harlan Howard's 'The Blizzard' is an edge-of-your-seat story-song delivered so convincingly that the listener forms a mental picture of Jim and his pony, Dan, fighting the elements as, frostbitten, the singer journeys home to his beloved Mary Ann.

The infectiously up-tempo 'Stand At Your Window,' also from 1961, was, like 'I'm Getting Better,' another double-sided hit for Reeves. But the other side, 'What Would You Do?,' is not included here. 'Four Walls,' a Number 11 pop hit, spent 8 consecutive weeks at Number 1 following its 1957 release, charting for a total of 26 weeks. 'Billy Bayou,' written by Roger Miller, a 1958 release and a Number 1 record for Jim, is a history lesson set to music, in much the same vein as Johnny Horton's recordings of 'The Battle of New Orleans,' 'Sink The Bismarck' and others.

'Am I Losing You,' a pensive ballad and another of Gentleman Jim's compositions, was the first of Reeves' five hits in 1957. The collection concludes with 'Danny Boy.' Never a hit for Jim, this public domain standard none the less bears the stamp of Reeves' own arrangement as he renders it in his rich baritone with the same sincerity as any Irish tenor.

KENNY ROGERS

TEN YEARS OF GOLD
EMI, 1988

THIS COLLECTION, WHICH REALLY EMPHASIZES ROGERS' PRE-COUNTRY CAREER WITH THE FIRST EDITION ROCK GROUP, charted for 61 weeks when it was released on vinyl by United Artists in 1977. As significantly, its success is largely responsible for Kenny's country career. While Rogers made the bottom of the country charts in 1973 with his recording of the country classic, 'Today I Started Lovin' You Again' and had a Top 20 hit in 1975 with the gospel-flavored 'Love Lifted Me' (both included here), it wasn't until 1977 that he found a home on the country charts with 'Lucille.' 'Lucille' was not only a gold record for Kenny, it was so widely heard that no one would make the mistake of thinking that he had recorded Little Richard's 1957 rocker of the same title.

Mel Tillis' composition, 'Ruby, Don't Take Your Love To Town,' was a country as well as a pop hit for Rogers And The First Edition in 1969, as was 'Ruben James.' 'But You Know I Love You,' written by First Edition member Mike Settles, was a folk-flavored hit in 1969. Mac Davis' 'Something's Burning,' a 1970 hit for Rogers' quintet, did not chart country, nor did the group's earliest pop hit 'Just Dropped In' (1968), an atypical Mickey Newbury composition.

'Daytime Friends,' Rogers' follow-up to 'Lucille,' was also a Number 1 country hit, though, like 'Lucille' and many of Kenny's country hits, it too crossed over to the pop charts. 'Daytime Friends,' riding on the momentum of 'Lucille,' proved that Rogers could faithfully render a cheatin' song.

Kenny's 1976 cover of 'While The Feeling's Good' is as good as Mike Lunsford's 1975 original, but the ungrammatical lyrics (for example, the reference to lips "that's burnin'") don't match the rest of the material on Ten Years Of Gold.

THE STATLER BROTHERS

BEST OF THE STATLER BROTHERS
Mercury, 1975

THIS PRE-JIMMY FORTUNE "GREATEST HITS" PACKAGE, FIRST RELEASED ON VINYL IN 1975, REMAINED ON *BILLBOARD*'S COUNTRY album chart for 12 weeks and features the original Statlers: Harold, Don, Phil and Lew.

'Bed Of Roses' is a coming-of-age narrative and the Statler Brothers' first hit for Mercury Records. 'Whatever Happened To Randolph Scott' waxes nostalgic about the cowboy movie heroes of yesteryear, while 'Do You Remember These' (1972) is probably the most clever of the quartet's nostalgic songs. It was banned in the UK because of a supposedly lewd reference to knickers (i.e. men's knee pants: in Britain, ladies' underwear).

'Carry Me Back' is a 1973 plea for a trip down memory lane. Next is 'Flowers On The Wall.' Released in 1965, this record was the Statler Brothers' first hit, a Top 5 country and pop record, and a novelty song that showed fans that the group had a comic bent along with its pitch-perfect musical harmony.

'The Class Of '57,' the group's 1972 follow-up to 'Do You Remember These,' is a bittersweet update on the lives of high school classmates. Don Reid's composition, 'I'll Go To My Grave Loving You,' an "earthy" declaration of fidelity speculating on the prospect of devotion beyond the grave, was a Top 5 hit for the Statlers in 1975. 'Pictures' is a 1971 look through the family scrapbook, once again evoking bittersweet memories.

'Thank You World' was the group's 1974 expression of gratitude to all those responsible for their success. 'New York City' is Don Reid's 1971 saga of a contrite unwed father, while another of his compositions, 'Susan When She Tried,' rounds out these sides.

GARY STEWART

OUT OF HAND
Hightone, 1991

OUT OF HAND REMAINED ON *BILLBOARD*'S COUNTRY ALBUM CHART FOR 30 WEEKS WHEN RCA FIRST RELEASED IT ON vinyl in 1975.

The title song, like most of Stewart's repertoire, is in the vein of the cheatin', drinkin' and hell-raisin' honky-tonk songs that typify what was once the most identifiable sound of country music.

With such limited subject-matter to draw on, Gary made the most of his abilities as a singer, musician and songwriter. His songs have been recorded by country stars Hank Snow, Del Reeves, Warner Mack, Cal Smith, Nat Stuckey, Johnny Paycheck, Kenny Price, Jack Greene and Billy Walker.

These sides feature Nashville's best pickers—including session leader Harold Bradley on bass guitar, drummer Buddy Harman, steel guitarists Weldon Myrick and Pete Drake, "harmonicat" Charlie McCoy and Gary on guitar and piano—along with two of Music City's best background vocal groups, the Jordanaires and the Nashville Edition.

Leading off with Stewart's first hit, Wayne Carson's 'Drinkin' Thing,' Gary then goes 'Honky-Tonkin'' (not a hit for Stewart). 'I See The Want To In Your Eyes,' another Wayne Carson song, is a cover of Conway Twitty's 1974 Number 1 hit, while 'This Old Heart Won't Let Go' is another recording Stewart never actually released as a single.

'Draggin' Shackles,' co-written by Gary Stewart and Nat Stuckey, is followed by another Wayne Carson composition, Gary's classic 1975 hit, 'She's Acting Single (I'm Drinking Doubles).' 'Back Sliders Wine' was first recorded by its writer, Michael Martin Murphey, in 1979 and is followed by 'Sweet Country Red' (the reference is to a woman), the title song, and 'Williamson County.'

HANK WILLIAMS

HEALTH AND HAPPINESS SHOWS
Mercury, 1993

THESE 1949 RADIO TRANSCRIPTIONS WERE TAKEN FROM 33 RPM 16-IN. ACETATE DISCS WHICH, NATURALLY, HAD surface noise. To preserve the integrity of the original recordings, featuring Hank, his wife, Audrey, Williams' Drifting Cowboy Band and legendary Grand Ole Opry announcer Grant Turner, no noise reduction techniques have been utilized.

Listeners are none the poorer, however, as they are treated to eight shows, each of which ran for approximately 12 minutes and featured such Hank hits such as 'Wedding Bells,' 'Lovesick Blues,' 'I'm A Long Gone Daddy,' 'Lost Highway,' 'A Mansion On The Hill,' 'Mind Your Own Business' and 'I'm So Lonesome I Could Cry.' There are also Williams versions of 'Old Joe Clark,' '(There's A) Bluebird On Your Windowsill,' 'Fire On The Mountain,' 'Bile Them Cabbage Down,' 'The Prodigal Son,' 'Pan American,' 'Arkansas Traveler' and 'Cotton-Eyed Joe,' and the opening and closing themes of the series—'Happy Rovin' Cowboy' and 'Sally Goodin' respectively.

The commercials for Hadacol, a terrible-tasting patent medicine, have been excised from these cuts, a blessing perhaps to a commercially satiated generation, but it would have been nice to hear at least one of these pitches for they, like early TV ads, might provide a cultural key for those of us born after 1949.

CD listings

The following list contains the main releases by the artists and bands described earlier in the book. The artists and bands are listed alphabetically, followed by their albums (also in alphabetical order). Each entry contains the name of the album and the year of the CD's release, followed by the record labels and catalogue numbers under which the albums have been released in CD format.

Some albums are currently unavailable on CD. Compilations containing the work of various artists are included at the end of the listing.

ROY ACUFF
The Best Of Roy Acuff
1991
US: CURB D2-77454
The Essential Roy Acuff (1936–1942)
1992
US: COLUMBIA COUNTRY CLASSIC LEGACY SERIES CK48956

ALABAMA
Alabama's Greatest Hits
1986
US: RCA PCD1-7170
UK: RCA PD87170
Feels So Right
1988
US: RCA PCD1-3930-R-E
Gonna Have A Party
1993
US: RCA 07863661492
Roll On
1988
US: RCA PCD1-4939
UK: RCA PD84939
The Touch
1988
US: RCA 07863-55649-2

BILL ANDERSON
Best Of Bill Anderson *1991*
US: CURB D2-77436
Country Music Heaven
1983
US: CURB D2-77593

EDDY ARNOLD
The Best Of Eddy Arnold
1967
US: RCA 3675-2-R
Cattle Call: There Hangs A Tale
1990
US: BEAR FAMILY RECORDS BCD15441
UK: BEAR FAMILY RECORDS BCD15441
You Don't Miss A Thing
1990
US: RCA 3020-2-R

CHET ATKINS
Chet Atkins Picks On The Hits
1989
US: RCA PDC2-1265
Pickin My Way—In Hollywood—Alone
1973
US: MOBILE FIDELITY MFCD-2-787

Street Dreams
1986
US: CBS CK40256

CHET ATKINS AND JERRY REED
Sneakin' Around
1992
US: COLUMBIA CK 47873

BOBBY BARE
Bobby Bare's Greatest Hits
1992
US: BAREWORKS BWCD
Bobby Bare: The Mercury Years (1970–1972): Part 1
1987
US: BEAR FAMILY RECORDS BCD 155417-1
Bobby Bare: The Mercury Years (1970–1972): Part 2
1987
US: BEAR FAMILY RECORDS 15417-2
Bobby Bare: The Mercury Years (1970–1972): Part 3
1987
US: BEAR FAMILY RECORDS BCD 15417-3

CLINT BLACK
The Hard Way
1992
US: RCA 66003-2
UK: RCA 7863 66003-2
Killin' Time
1989
US: RCA 9688-2-R
UK: RCA PD 90443
Put Yourself In My Shoes *1990*
US: RCA 23272-2-R
UK: RCA PD 90544

GARTH BROOKS
Beyond The Season
1992
US: LIBERTY C2-98742
UK: CAPITOL CDP7987422
The Chase *1992*
US: LIBERTY C2-98743
UK: LIBERTY CD ESTU 2184
Garth Brooks *1989*
US: LIBERTY C2-90897
UK: CAPITOL CZ304
Ropin' The Wind
1991
US: LIBERTY C2-96330
UK: CAPITOL CD ESTU 2162

JIM ED BROWN AND HELEN CORNELIUS
Jim Ed Brown and Helen Cornelius' Greatest Hits *1988*
US: RCA 07863-55279-2

GLEN CAMPBELL
Best Of The Early
Years
1991
US: Curb/Capitol D2-77441
The Glen
Campbell Story
1987
US: K-Tel ONCD-5112
UK: K-Tel ONCD-5112
Greatest Country
Hits
1990
US: Curb/Capitol D2-77362

**MARY-CHAPIN
CARPENTER**
State Of The Heart
1989
US: CBS CK44228
UK: CBS 466691-2
Shooting Straight In
The Dark
1992
US: CBS CK46077
UK: Columbia 467468-2
Come On, Come On
1992
US: Columbia CK 48881
UK: Columbia 471898-2

CARTER FAMILY
The Bristol Sessions
1991
US: The Country Music
Foundation CMF-011-D

The Carter Family:
Country Music Hall
Of Fame Series
1991
US: MCA Records
MCAD 10088
Clinch Mountain
Treasures
1991
US: County Records
CCS CD 112
Diamond In The
Rough *1990*
US: Copper Creek
Records 0107

JOHNNY CASH
Best of Johnny Cash
1991
US: Curb D2-77494
UK: Starlite CDS 51010
Boom Chicka Boom
1990
US: Mercury 842 155-2
UK: Mercury 842 755-2
Classic Cash
1988
US: Mercury 834-526-2
UK: Mercury 834526-2
Up Through The
Years 1955–1957
1986
US: Bear Family Records
04794-1399
UK: Bear Family Records
BCD-15247

ROSANNE CASH
Interiors
1990
US: Columbia CK46079
Seven Year Ache
1981
US: Columbia CK36965
The Wheel
1993
US: Columbia CK 52729

ROY CLARK
The Best Of
Roy Clark
1990
US: Curb D2-77395
Roy Clark Live
In Branson,
Missouri, USA
1993
US: Delta 12135

PATSY CLINE
12 Greatest Hits
1988
US: MCA Records MCAD-12
UK: MCA Records
DMCL-1875
The Last Sessions
1988
US: MCA Records
MCAD 25199
Patsy Cline At Her
Best *1992*
US: Highland Music
HCD 464

The Patsy Cline
Collection
1991
US: MCA Records
MCAD4-10421
Patsy Cline Live
At The Opry
1988
US: MCA Records
MCAD 42142
UK: MCA Records
DMCL-1891

EARL THOMAS CONLEY
The Heart Of It All
1988
US: RCA 6824-2-R
UK: RCA PD86824
Greatest Hits
1985
US: RCA PCD1-7032-RE
UK: RCA ND90314
Greatest Hits
Volume 2
1990
US: RCA 2043-2R

BILLY RAY CYRUS
In The Heart Of A
Woman
1993
US: Mercury 314-514-758-2
UK: Mercury 510635-2
Some Gave All
1992
US: Mercury 314-510-635-2

CHARLIE DANIELS
Charlie Daniels All
Time Greatest Hits
1992
US: Epic EK53743
Renegade *1991*
US: Epic 46835

**CHARLIE DANIELS
BAND**
A Decade Of Hits
1983
US: Epic EK 38795

**SKEETER DAVIS AND
NRBQ**
She Sings, They Play
1986
US: Rounder CD 3092

JIMMY DEAN
24 Greatest Hits
1989
US: Highland DCD 7860
Country Spotlight
1991
US: Dominion 30042

FREDDY FENDER
20 Greatest Hits
1989
US: Highland HCD 407
UK: Big Country 263001-2
The Freddy Fender
Collection *1991*
US: Reprise 9-26638-2

ERNIE FORD
16 Tons Of Boogie:
The Best Of
Tennessee Ernie
Ford
1990
US: RHINO R2 79975
Country Gospel
Classic Volume 2
1991
US: CAPITOL C2 95915
Red, White And
Blue
1991
US: CAPITOL C2-96677
Songs Of The Civil
War
1991
US: CAPITOL C2-7-95705-2

LEFTY FRIZZELL
The Best Of Lefty
Frizzell
1991
US: RHINO R2-71005

CRYSTAL GAYLE
Best Always
1993
US: BRANSON ENTERTAINMENT
BRD9307
The Best Of Crystal
Gayle
1986
US: WARNER BROTHERS 999-
25622-2

UK: WARNER BROTHERS
925622-2
Crystal Gayle's All
Time Greatest Hits
1990
US: CURB D2-77380
Greatest Hits *1991*
US: CAPITOL C2-95886

DON GIBSON
18 Greatest Hits
1990
US: CURB D2-77474
The Best Of Don
Gibson: Volume 1
1991
US: CURB D2-77440
Country Spotlight
1992
US: DOMINION 3082-2
A Legend In My
Time
1987
US: BEAR FAMILY RECORDS
BCD 15401
UK: BEAR FAMILY RECORDS
BCD 15401

VINCE GILL
The Best of Vince
Gill *1989*
US: RCA 9814-2-R
I Never Knew
Lonely
1988
US: RCA 07863-61130-2

I Still Believe In
You
1992
US: MCA RECORDS
MCAD-10630
UK: MCA RECORDS
MCAD-10630
Pocketful Of Gold
1991
US: MCA RECORDS
MCAD-10140
UK: MCA RECORDS
MCAD-10140
When I Call Your
Name *1989*
US: MCA RECORDS
MCAD-42321

JACK GREENE
Sings His Best
1982
US: STEP ONE EMH 1003-CD

NANCI GRIFFITH
The Last Of The
True Believers
1986
US: ROUNDER ROPH 1109
UK: DEMON REUCD 1013
Late Night
Grande Hotel
1991
US: MCA RECORDS
MCAD 10306
UK: MCA RECORDS
MCAD 10304

Lone Star State
Of Mind
1987
US: MCA RECORDS
MCAD 31300
UK: MCA RECORDS
MCAD
1976
Other Voices, Other
Rooms
1993
US: ELEKTRA 9614-2
UK: MCA RECORDS
MCAD 10796

MERLE HAGGARD
18 Rare Classics
1991
US: CURB D2-77490
Blue Jungle
1990
US: CURB D2-77313
I'm Always On
A Mountain When
I Fall
1986
US: MCA RECORDS
MCAD 1644
Merle Haggard's
Greatest Hits
1982
US: MCA RECORDS
MCAD 5386
More Of The Best
1989
US: RHINO R2 70917

There's A Light
Beyond These
Woods
1986
US: ROUNDER ROPH 1097

EMMYLOU HARRIS
Pieces Of The Sky
1975
US: REPRISE 2284-2
Profile: The Best Of
Emmylou Harris
1978
US: WARNER BROTHERS 3258-2
UK: WARNER BROTHERS
256570
Profile II: The Best
Of Emmylou Harris
1984
US: WARNER BROTHERS 9
25161-2

**EMMYLOU HARRIS
AND THE NASH
RAMBLERS**
Emmylou Harris
And The Nash
Ramblers At The
Ryman
1992
US: REPRISE 9-26664-2
UK: REPRISE 7599-26664-2

ALAN JACKSON
Don't Rock The
Jukebox

1991
US: ARISTA ARCD 8681
**Here In The Real
World**
1991
US: ARISTA ARCD 8623
UK: ARISTA ARCD 260817
**A Lot About Livin'
(And A Little
'Bout Love)**
1992
US: ARISTA 07822-18911-2

SONNY JAMES
American Originals
1989
US: COLUMBIA 45066
**The Best Of
Sonny James**
1991
US: CURB D2-77460
Greatest Hits
1990
US: CURB D2-77359
Young Love
1992
US: PAIR PCD-1310

WAYLON JENNINGS
**The Taker, Tulsa
and Honky Tonk
Heroes**
1973
US: MOBILE FIDELITY MFCD 779
The Eagle
1990

US: EPIC EK 46104
UK: SONY MUSIC 467260-2
Hangin' Tough
1987
US: MCA RECORDS
MCAD 31298
UK: MCA RECORDS
DMCF 3360

**WAYLON JENNINGS,
WILLIE NELSON, JESSI
COLTER AND TOMPALL
GLASER**
**Wanted: The
Outlaws**
1988
US: RCA RECORDS 5976-2-R

GEORGE JONES
**George Jones'
Greatest Country
Hits**
1990
US: CURB D2-77369
One Woman Man
1989
US: EPIC 44078
UK: SONY MUSIC 465186-2
Walls Can Fall
1993
US: MCA RECORDS
MCAD 10652

KRIS KRISTOFFERSON
**Jesus Was A
Capricorn**

1991
US: SONY AK 47064
**Live At The
Philharmonic**
1992
US: SONY AK 52415
**The Silver Tongued
Devil And I**
1988
US: CBS AK 44352

K. D. LANG
**Shadowland (The
Owen Bradley
Sessions)**
1988
US: SIRE 9-25724-2
UK: MCA RECORDS
WX171
Angel With A Lariat
1987
US: SIRE 25441-2

**K.D. LANG AND THE
RECLINES**
**Absolute Torch and
Twang**
1989
US: SIRE 9-25887-2
UK: WEA WX-259

LITTLE TEXAS
Big Time
1993
US: WARNER BROTHERS
9-45276-2

**First Time For
Everything**
1992
US: WARNER BROTHERS
9-26820-2
UK: WARNER BROTHERS
7599-26820-2

LOUVIN BROTHERS
The Louvin Brothers
1972
US: CAPITOL TOCP-6432

LYLE LOVETT
Joshua Judges Ruth
1992
US: MCA/CURB
MCAD 10475
UK: MCA MCAD 10475

LORETTA LYNN
Loretta Lynn
1987
US: MCA RECORDS
MCAD-5943
**Loretta Lynn:
Country Music Hall
of Fame Series**
1991
US: MCA RECORDS
MCAD 10083
**You Ain't Woman
Enough**
1991
US: MCA RECORDS
MCAD 22041

REBA MCENTIRE
**The Best Of Reba
McEntire**
1980
US: MERCURY RECORDS
824342-2
**For My Broken
Heart**
1991
US: MCA RECORDS
MCAD 10400
UK: MCA RECORDS
MCAD 10400
It's Your Call
1993
US: MCA RECORDS
MCAD 10673
Reba Live *1989*
US: MCA RECORDS MCAD
8034
Rumor Has It
1990
US: MCA RECORDS
MCAD 10016
**What Am I Going
To Do Without You**
1986
US: MCA RECORDS
MCAD 5807

BARBARA MANDRELL
**Barbara Mandrell's
Greatest Hits**
1985
US: MCA RECORDS
MCAD 31302

The Best Of Barbara Mandrell
1979
US: MCA RECORDS
MCAD 31107

ROGER MILLER
The Best Of Roger Miller Volume One: Country Tunesmith
1991
US: POLYGRAM 848-977-2
Country Spotlight
1991
US: DOMINION 30062
King Of The Road
1992
US: EPIC EK 53017

RONNIE MILSAP
Back To The Grindstone
1991
US: RCA 2375-2-R
Greatest Hits Volume 2
1985
US: RCA PCD1-5421
Heart And Soul
1987
US: RCA 7618-2-R
Lost In The Fifties Tonight
1986
US: RCA PCD-7194
Stranger Things

Have Happened
1989
US: RCA 9588-2-R

BILL MONROE
Columbia Historic Edition
1984
US: CBS CK 38904

BILL MONROE AND THE BLUE GRASS BOYS
Bill Monroe And The Bluegrass Boys Live At The Opry
1989
US: MCA RECORDS
MCAD 42286
Southern Flavor
1988
US: MCA RECORDS
MCAD 42133

GEORGE MORGAN
American Originals
1990
US: COLUMBIA CK 45076

LORRIE MORGAN
Classics
1991
US: CURB D2-77470
Something In Red
1991
US: RCA 3021-2-R
UK: RCA PD 90560

Tell Me I'm Dreaming
1992
US: INTERSONG CDA 5009
Watch Me *1992*
US: BNA 078863 666047-2

WILLIE NELSON
The Best of Willie Nelson *1992*
US: RCA RECORDS 56335-2
Greatest Hits And Rare Tracks (1959–1971)
1990
US: RHINO R2 70987
Shotgun Willie *1988*
US: ATLANTIC 7262-2

WILLIE NELSON, WAYLON JENNINGS, JOHNNY CASH AND KRIS KRISTOFFERSON
The Highwayman
1985
US: COLUMBIA CK 40056
Highwayman 2
1990
US: CBS RECORDS CK 45240
UK: COLUMBIA 466652-2

NITTY GRITTY DIRT BAND
Circle II–20 Song Collection *1989*
US: UNIVERSAL UVLD 72500

Nitty Gritty Dirt Band Live Two Five
1991
US: CAPITOL/NASHVILLE C293128
Will The Circle Be Unbroken: Volume 1
1985
US: EMI E246589

OAK RIDGE BOYS
Greatest Hits
1985
US: MCA MCAD 5150
Greatest Hits 2
1984
US: MCA MCAD 5496
UK: MCA MCAD 5496

K. T. OSLIN
Eighties Ladies
1987
US: RCA 2193-2-R
UK: RCA PD85924
Love In A Small Town *1990*
US: RCA 2365-2-R
UK: RCA PD90545
Songs From An Aging Sex Bomb
1993
US: RCA 66227-2
This Woman
1988
US: RCA 8369-2-R
UK: RCA PD88369

MARIE OSMOND
All In Love *1988*
US: CAPITOL C2-48968
UK: EMI CDP748968-2
I Only Wanted You
1986
US: CAPITOL CDP 7-46346-2
UK: EMI CDP746348-2
There's No Stopping Your Heart
1985
US: CAPITOL C21K-7-4849-2

PAUL OVERSTREET
Heroes *1990*
US: RCA 2459-2-R
Sowin' Love
1992
US: RCA 9617-2-R

BUCK OWENS
Buck Owens' All Time Greatest Hits Volume One
1990
US: CURB/CAPITOL D2-77342
Buck Owens' All Time Greatest Hits Volume Two
1992
US: CURB D2 77568
The Buck Owens Collection (1959–1990)
1992
US: RHINO R2 71016

Live At
Carnegie Hall
1988
US: CMF-012-D

DOLLY PARTON
The Best There Is
1987
US: RCA 6497-2-RRE
Slow Dancing With
The Moon
1993
US: COLUMBIA CK 53199
UK: COLUMBIA 472944-2
White Limozeen
1989
US: CBS CK 44384
UK: CBS CK 465135-2
The World Of Dolly
Parton Volume Two
1988
US: CBS AK44362

**DOLLY PARTON, LINDA
RONSTADT AND
EMMYLOU HARRIS**
Trio
1987
US: WARNER BROTHERS
9-25491-2

**DOLLY PARTON AND
PORTER WAGONER**
Sweet Harmony
1992
US: PAIR PDC2-1013

JOHNNY PAYCHECK
Country Spotlight
1991
US: DOMINION 30052
Greatest Hits
1987
US: EPIC EK38322
Live In Branson
Missouri USA
1993
US: DELTA 12163

RAY PRICE
The Essential
Ray Price:
1951–1962
1991
US: COLUMBIA CK 48532
Greatest Hits
Volume IV
1989
US: STEP ONE SOR 0050

CHARLEY PRIDE
The Best Of Charley
Pride
1988
US: RCA 5968-2-R
Greatest Hits
1988
US: RCA 6917-2-R

JIM REEVES
16 Greatest Songs
1990
US: RCA CD 11015

The Best Of Jim
Reeves Volume III
1989
US: RCA CAMDEN CLASSICS
CADI-2702
He'll Have To Go
And Other Favorites
1988
US: RCA 07863-52301-2

JEANNIE C. RILEY
Jeannie C.
1991
US: PLAYBACK PCD 4502

TEX RITTER
Best Of The Country
1988
US: HIGHLAND NCD 2148
Tex Ritter's Greatest
Hits
1990
US: CURB D2 77397-2

MARTY ROBBINS
American Originals
1990
US: COLUMBIA CK45069
The Essential Marty
Robbins 1951–1982
1991
US: COLUMBIA CK 48537
Isle Of Golden
Dreams
1992
US: SONY A 1880

Marty Robbins'
Greatest Hits *1987*
US: COLUMBIA CK 38309

JIMMIE RODGERS
The Early Years
1991
US: ROUNDER ROCD 1057
No Hard Times
1991
US: ROUNDER ROCD 1062
UK: ROUNDER ROCD 1062
On The Way Up
1991
US: ROUNDER ROCD 1058
UK: ROUNDER CDROU 01058

KENNY ROGERS
Back Home Again
1991
US: REPRISE 26740-2
If Only My Heart
Had A Voice
1993
US: GIANT 9-21490-2
Kenny Rogers'
Greatest Hits *1988*
US: RCA 8371-2-R-1
Love Is Strange
1990
US: REPRISE 26289-2
They Don't Make
Them Like They
Used To *1986*
US: RCA 5633-2-R
UK: RCA PD85855

ROY ROGERS
The Best Of Roy
Rogers
1990
US: CURB D2-77392
Roy Rogers:
Country Music Hall
Of Fame Series
1992
US: MCA RECORDS
MCAD 10548
Roy Rogers' Tribute
1991
US: RCA CD-0-3024-3R

SAWYER BROWN
Cafe On The Corner
1992
US: CURB D-2 77574
The Dirt Road
1992
US: CURB/CAPITOL C2 85624
Somewhere In
The Night
1987
US: CAPITOL CCT 746923-2

RICKY SKAGGS
Highways And
Heartaches
1982
US: EPIC EK 37996
Love's Gonna Get Ya
1986
US: EPIC EK 40309
UK: EPIC CDEPC 57095

**Favorite Country
Songs**
1985
US: Epic EK 39409
UK: Epic 982587-2

HANK SNOW
**Collectors Series
Volume 2**
1992
US: RCA 07863 5227902
**All Time Greatest
Hits**
1990
US: RCA 996829
Snow Country
1992
US: Pair PCD2-1314

STATLER BROTHERS
**The Statler
Brothers' Greatest
Hits**
1988
US: Mercury 934-626-2

RAY STEVENS
**I Never Made A
Reord I Didn't Like**
1988
US: MCA Records
MCAD 42172
**Ray Stevens'
Greatest Hits**
1983
US: RCA 5153-2-R

**Ray Stevens'
Greatest Hits**
1991
US: Curb D2 77464

GARY STEWART
Battleground
1990
US: Hightone HCD 8014
Brand New
1990
US: Hightone HCD 8014
Gary's Greatest
1991
US: Hightone HCD8030

DOUG STONE
Doug Stone
1990
US: Epic EK 45303
From The Heart
1992
US: Epic EK 47357
**I Thought It Was
You** *1991*
US: Epic EK 47357
UK: Epic 468822-2

GEORGE STRAIT
**Chill Of An
Early Fall**
1991
US: MCA Records
MCAD 10204
UK: MCA Records
MCAD 10214

Livin' It Up
1990
US: MCA Records
MCAD 6415
Strait Country
1981
US: MCA Records
MCAD 31087

MARTY STUART
Hillbilly Rock
1989
US: MCA Records
MCAD 42312
**Let There Be
Country**
1992
US: Columbia CK 40829
Tempted
1991
US: MCA Records
MCAD 10106
**This One's Gonna
Hurt You**
1992
US: MCA Records
MCAD 10596

HANK THOMPSON
**All Time Greatest
Hits** *1990*
US: Curb D2-77329
Hank Thompson
1992
US: MCA Records
MCAD 10545

**The Hank
Thompson Country
Collection**
1991
UK: Knight Records
KNCD 13059

MEL TILLIS
American Originals
1990
US: Columbia CK 45079
Greatest Hits
1991
US: Curb D2 77482

PAM TILLIS
**Homeward Looking
Angel**
1992
US: Arista 18649-2
**Put Yourself In
My Place**
1991
US: Arista ARCD 8642

AARON TIPPIN
**Read Between The
Lines**
1992
US: RCA 07863
**You've Got To
Stand For
Something**
1990
US: RCA 2374-2-R
UK: RCA PD82374

MERLE TRAVIS
**The Best Of Merle
Travis**
1990
US: Rhino R2-70993

RANDY TRAVIS
Always And Forever
1987
US: Warner Brothers
9-25568-2
UK: WEA 925568-2
**Greatest Hits
Volume 1**
1992
US: Warner Brothers
9-45044-2
Heroes And Friends
1990
US: Warner Brothers
9-26310-2
Old 8 X 10 *1988*
US: Warner Brothers
9-25738-2
UK: Warner Brothers
9-254•5-2
Storms Of Life *1986*
US: Warner Brothers
254352
UK: WEA 925435-2

TRAVIS TRITT
Country Club
1990
US: Warner Brothers
9-26094-2

It's All About To Change
1991
US: WARNER BROTHERS
9-26589-2

ERNEST TUBB
Ernest Tubb:
Country Music Hall
of Fame Series
1991
US: MCA RECORDS
MCAD 10086
Ernest Tubb Live
(1965) *1989*
US: RHINO R2-70902
The Legend And
Friends
1992
US: LASERLIGHT 12119

TANYA TUCKER
Can't Run From
Yourself
1992
US: LIBERTY CDP-7-98987-2
UK: LIBERTY CDP-7-98987-2
Greatest Country
Hits *1991*
US: CURB D2-77429
Greatest Hits *1989*
US: CAPITOL CDP 7 01814 2
What Do I Do
With Me
1991
US: CAPITOL C2 95562

CONWAY TWITTY
#1s *1976*
US: MCA RECORDS
MCAD 32140
Conway Twitty's
Greatest Hits:
Volume I
1972
US: MCA RECORDS
MCAD 31239
Conway Twitty's
Greatest Hits:
Volume II
1976
US: MCA RECORDS
MCAD 31240
Crazy In Love
1990
US: MCA RECORDS
MCAD 10027

PORTER WAGONER
Heartwarming
Songs *1990*
US: HIGHLAND HCD-419

BILLY WALKER
Greatest Hits On
Monument
1993
US: SONY/CBS AK 52963

KITTY WELLS
Greatest Hits
Volume 1 *1989*
US: STEP ONE SOR 0046

Greatest Hits
Volume 2
1989
US: STEP ONE SOR 0047
Kitty Wells: Country
Music Hall Of Fame
Series
1991
US: MCA RECORDS
MCAD 10081
Queen Of Country
Music
1992
US: DELTA MUSIC 15484

DOTTIE WEST
Dottie West's
Greatest Hits
1992
US: CURB D2-77555

DON WILLIAMS
The Best Of Don
Wiliams Volume 2
1979
US: MCA RECORDS
MCAD 31172
Currents
1992
US: RCA 61128-2
UK: RCA PD90645
Don Williams'
Greatest Country
Hits
1990
US: CURB D2-77361

Don Williams'
Greatest Hits
Volume 4
1985
US: MCA RECORDS
MCAD-31248
One Good Well
1989
US: RCA 9656-2-R
True Love
1990
US: RCA 2407-2-R
UK: RCA PD90538

HANK WILLIAMS
40 Greatest Hits
1978
US: POLYDOR 821-233-2
I Won't Be Home
No More:
June 1952–
September 1952
1987
US: POLYDOR 833752-2
Rare Demos: First
To Last
1990
US: COUNTRY MUSIC
FOUNDATION RECORDS
CMF 067-D

HANK WILLIAMS, JR.
The Best Of Hank
Williams, Jr.
1991
US: CURB D2-77418

The Bocephus Box:
The Hank Williams,
Jr. Collection
1979–1992
1992
US: CURB/CAPRICORN
9-45104-2
Hank Williams, Jr.'s
Greatest Hits
Volume 2
1984
US: CURB 25328-2
Out Of Left Field
1993
US: CURB/CAPRICORN
9-45225-2
Roots And Ranches
1991
US: POLYGRAM 8485752

TAMMY WYNETTE
Heart Over Mind
1990
US: CBS 46238
UK: EPIC 467355-2
Higher Ground
1987
US: EPIC EK 40832
UK: EPIC 451148-2
Tammy Wynette's
Best Loved Hits
1991
US: EPIC EK 48588
Tammy Wynette's
Biggest *1991*
US: EPIC EK38312

WYNONNA
Wynonna
1992
US: CURB/MCA MCAD-10529

TRISHA YEARWOOD
Hearts In Armor
1992
US: MCA RECORDS MCAD 10641
UK: MCA RECORDS MCAD 10641
Trisha Yearwood
1991
US: MCA RECORDS MCAD 10297
UK: MCA RECORDS MCAD 10297

DWIGHT YOAKAM
Guitars, Cadillacs, Etc.
1986
US: REPRISE 9-25-372-2
UK: REPRISE 9-25-372-2
Just Lookin' For A Hit
1989
US: REPRISE 9-25982-2
UK: WEA 9-25982-2
If There Was A Way
1990
US: REPRISE 9-26344-2
UK: WEA 759926334-2

This Time
1993
US: REPRISE 9-452-41-2
UK: WEA 936245241-2

FARON YOUNG
Here's To You
1988
US: STEP ONE RECORDS SOR 0040

FARON YOUNG AND RAY PRICE
Memories That Last
1991
US: STEP ONE RECORDS SOR 0068

COMPILATIONS

Classic Country
1991
US: RHINO PRO2-90089

Columbia Country Classics Volume 1
1990
US: COLUMBIA CK 46029

Columbia Country Classics Volume 2
1990
US: COLUMBIA CK 46030

Columbia Country

Classics Volume 3
1990
US: COLUMBIA CK 46031

Columbia Country Classics Volume 4
1990
US: COLUMBIA CK 46032

Columbia Country Classics Volume 5
1990
US: COLUMBIA CK 46033

The Firm: Original Motion Picture Soundtrack
1993
US: MCA RECORDS MCAD 2007

Bibliography

Allen, Bob: *George Jones: The Saga of An American Singer,* Dolphin, 1984.

Anderson, Bill: *Whisperin' Bill,* Longstreet Press, 1989.

Arnold, Eddy: *It's A Long Way From Chester County,* Hewitt House, 1969.

Bronson, Fred: *The Billboard Book of Number One Hits,* Billboard, 1985.

Brooks, Tim and Earle Marsh: *The Complete Directory To Prime Time Network TV Shows,* Ballantine Books, 1981.

Campbell, Archie: *Archie Campbell: An Autobiography,* Memphis State University Press, 1981.

Cantwell, Robert: *Bluegrass Breakdown,* University of Illinois Press, 1984.

Carr, Patrick (ed.): *The Illustrated History of Country Music,* Doubleday/Dolphin, 1979.

Cornfield, Robert: *Just Country,* McGraw-Hill, 1976.

Country Music Who's Who, Record World, 1972.

Cross, Wilbur and Michael Kosser: *The Conway Twitty Story,* Dolphin, 1986.

Cusic, Don: *Randy Travis: The King of the New Country Traditionalists,* St. Martin's Press, 1990.

Cusic, Don: *Reba: Country Music's Queen,* St. Martin's Press, 1991.

Eatherly, Pat Travis: *In Search of My Father,* Broadman Press, 1987.

Emery, Ralph: *Memories: The*

Autobiography of Ralph Emery, Macmillan, 1991.

Eng, Steve: *A Satisfied Mind,* Rutledge Hill Press, 1992.

Eremo, Judie (ed.): *Country Musicians,* Grove Press, 1987.

Gaillard, Frye: *Watermelon Wine,* St. Martin's Press, 1978.

Garcia, Guy: 'Scoot Your Booty,' *Time,* March 15, 1993, pp. 60–2.

Graham, David: *He Walks With Me,* Simon & Schuster, 1977.

Gray, Andy: *Great Country Music Stars,* Hamlyn, 1975.

Guralnick, Peter: *Lost Highway: Journeys and Arrivals of American Musicians,* David R. Godine, 1979.

Hall, Tom T.: *The Storyteller's Nashville,* Doubleday, 1979.

Harris, Stacy: *Comedians of Country Music,* Lerner Publishing, 1978.

Harris, Stacy: *The Carter Family,* Lerner

Publishing, 1978.

Hollaran, Carolyn Rada: *Meet the Stars of Country Music,* Aurora, 1977.

Hollaran, Carolyn Rada: *Our Brightest Stars of Country Music,* Nashville Celebrity Book Publishers, 1987.

Horstman, Dorothy: *Sing Your Heart Out Country Boy,* Country Music Foundation Press, 1986.

Lomax, John, III: *Nashville: Music City USA,* Harry N. Abrams, Inc. 1985.

Lord, Bobby: *Hit the Glory Road,* Broadman Press, 1969.

Lynn, Loretta: *Coal Miner's Daughter,* Henry Regnery, 1976.

Malone, Bill C. (ed.): *Stars of Country Music,* University of Illinois Press, 1975.

Malone, Bill: *Country Music USA,* University of Texas Press, 1985.

Mandrell, Barbara with George

Vecsey: *Get to the Heart: My Story ,* Bantam Books, 1990.

Mason, Michael (ed.): *The Country Music Book,* Charles Scribners Sons, 1985.

Milsap, Ronnie: *Almost Like A Song,* McGraw-Hill, 1990.

Nash, Alanna: *Beyond Closed Doors,* Knopf, 1988.

Nash, Alanna: *Dolly,* Reed Books, 1978.

Nelson, Susie: *Heart Worn Memories,* Eakin Press, 1987.

Nite, Norm N.: *Rock On: The Solid Gold Years,* Harper & Row, 1982.

Nite, Norm N.: *Rock On: Volume Two,* Crowell, 1982.

Oak Ridge Boys: *The Oak Ridge Boys: Our Story,* Contemporary Books, 1987.

Pearl, Minnie: *Minnie Pearl: An Autobiography,* Pocket Books, 1982.

Pulse, April 1993, Page 13.

Riley, Jeannie C.:

From Harper Valley to the Mountaintop, Chosen Books, 1978.

Rogers, Kenny: *Making It With Music,* Harper & Row, 1978.

Rosenberg, Neil V.: *Bluegrass: A History,* University of Illinois Press, 1985.

Schlappi, Elizabeth: *Roy Acuff: The Smoky Mountain Boy,* Pelican, 1978.

Scobey, Lola: *Willie Nelson: Country Outlaw,* Zebra Books, 1982.

Selvia, Joel: *Ricky Nelson: Idol for a Generation,* Contemporary Books, 1990.

Strobel, Jerry (ed.): *Grand Ole Opry History Picture Book,* Opryland USA Inc, 1992.

Toshes, Nick: *Country: The Biggest Music In America,* Stein & Day, 1977.

Whitburn, Joel: *Joel Whitburn's Top Country Singles 1944–1988,* Record Research Inc, 1989.

White, Howard with Ruth White: *Every Highway Out of Nashville,* JMP Publications, 1990.

Williams, Hank, Jr: *Living Proof: An Autobiography,* G. P. Putnam's Sons, 1979.

index

Page numbers in italics refer to captions to illustrations

acknowledgements

AUTHOR'S ACKNOWLEDGEMENTS

Special thanks to Martin Corteel, Debbie Holley, Edward Morris, the Country Music Foundation's Head of Reference Ronnie Pugh (without whose help I could not have written The Best of Country), the CMF's Jane Messmore, Erin Morris, Cecilia Tichi, Melvin Sloan, Billy Walker, the Country Music Association's Gina Smith and everyone at Tower Records and The Ernest Tubb Record Shops for their assistance.

PICTURE ACKNOWLEDGEMENTS

Photographs reproduced by kind permission of London Features International/Rogan Coles, Bruce Kramer, Kevin Mazur, Gary Merrin, Ilpo Musto, Michael Ochs Archive, Tom Sheehan, Ron Wolfson; Redferns/Glenn A. Baker, Gary Brandon, Beth Gwinn, David Redfern, Ebet Roberts, Roger Sealy.

Front jacket: Retna/Jay Blakesberg
Back jacket: Rex Features; Pictorial Press; Pictorial Press/Keuntje; Rex Features; Retna/Michael Putland.